D0371352

Published by The Disinformation Company Ltd.
163 Third Avenue, Suite 108, New York, NY 10003 / Tel.: +1.212.691.1605 / Fax: +1.212.473.8096
www.disinfo.com

Design & Layout: Rebecca Meek

Library of Congress Control Number: 2004110503

ISBN 1-932857-02-8

Printed in the USA

Distributed in the USA and Canada by: Consortium Book Sales and Distribution
1045 Westgate Drive, Suite 90, St Paul, MN 55114 / Toll Free: +1.800.283.3572 / Local: +1.651.221.9035 / Fax: +1.651.221.0124 / www.cbsd.com

Distributed in the United Kingdom and Eire by: Turnaround Publisher Services Ltd.,
Unit 3, Olympia Trading Estate, Coburg Road, London, N22 6TZ / Tel.: +44.(0)20.8829.3000 / Fax: +44.(0)20.8881.5088 / www.turnaround-uk.com

Attention colleges and universities, corporations and other organizations:
Quantity discounts are available on bulk purchases of this book for educational training purposes, fund-raising,
or gift-giving. Special books, booklets, or book excerpts can also be created to fit your specific needs.
For information contact the Marketing Department of The Disinformation Company Ltd.

Disinformation is a registered trademark of The Disinformation Company Ltd.

10 9 8 7 6 5 4 3 2 1

5O THINGS YOU'RE NOT SUPPOSED TO KNOW

2

RUSS KICK

CONTENTS

CONTENTS

ABOUT THE AUTHOR

Besides the books opposite, Russ has written articles and a column for the *Village Voice* and several independent magazines. The Memory Hole [www.thememoryhole.org], a website devoted to rescuing knowledge and freeing information, is his labor of love.

Russ made world headlines in April 2004 when his Freedom of Information Act request/appeal resulted in the release of 288 photos of the US war dead coming home in flag-draped coffins. He posted the Pentagon-banned images on The Memory Hole, and overnight the story jumped into heavy rotation on the 24-hour news channels. The photos were carried by almost every newspaper in the world, often on the front page, and Russ was interviewed on *Good Morning America* and *CBS Evening News with Dan Rather*, plus numerous print outlets and NPR. The *Los Angeles Times* declared: "A new media player is born," while *Time*, in an article about blogs (even though The Memory Hole isn't a blog), asked: "How are you going to keep anything secret from a thousand Russ Kicks?"

The previous Halloween, Russ had made the front page of the *New York Times* when he digitally uncensored a heavily redacted Justice Department report.

Books

- *Outposts: A Catalogue of Rare and Disturbing Alternative Information* (author)

- *Psychotropedia: Publications from the Periphery* (author)

- *Hot Off the Net: Erotica and Other Sex Writings From the Internet* (editor)

- *You Are Being Lied To: The Disinformation Guide to Media Distortion, Historical Whitewashes and Cultural Myths* (editor)

- *Everything You Know Is Wrong: The Disinformation Guide to Secrets and Lies* (editor)

- *Abuse Your Illusions: The Disinformation Guide to Media Mirages and Establishment Lies* (editor)

- *50 Things You're Not Supposed to Know* (author)

- *The Disinformation Book of Lists* (author)

What turns a fact into something "you're not supposed to know"? Basically, it happens when that piece of information is upsetting, embarrassing, discomforting, or even damaging to a powerful party. The list of such parties is long — leaders of nations, legislatures, militaries, intelligence agencies, justice systems, regulatory agencies, corporations, mainstream media, the medical establishment, the educational system, religious institutions, racial and gender groups, academics and scholars in various disciplines, guardians of public morality, followers of ideologies, hypersenstitive leftists, conformist rightists, and others.

Other resistance comes from the fact that every historical figure has developed a cult of worshippers and cheerleaders who utterly refuse — in the face of all evidence — to admit the failings, hypocrisies, and, in some cases, the outright fraudulence of their idol.

In other cases, a fact doesn't offend an easily pinpointable institution or group. Instead, it's taboo because it exposes societal lies, the fables we tell ourselves in order to sugarcoat harsh reality.

With this in mind, it's time to present a second cavalcade of troublesome facts, compressed and boiled down to their very essences so that you can quickly digest them in an info-glutted world. For further explorations, references are given in the back. ☐

Acknowledgments

Thanks to Anne, my parents, Ruthanne, Jennifer, Billy Dale, Brett & Cristy, Darrell, Terry & Rebekah, Mike, Matt, Gary, Richard, Alex, Rebecca, Jason, Disinfo, and others who've slipped my overstuffed mind at the moment.

01
MEN HAVE CLITORISES

It's long been noted that all of us start in the womb as sexless little blobs. We each had the same undifferentiated external equipment (a bud of tissue), plus two sets of internal ducts.

Depending on whether an embryo has a Y sex chromosome or two X's, during week seven it starts developing into a boy or a girl. That little mound of tissue (the genital tubercle) either opens to form two sets of labia and a clitoris, or it closes to make a penis and testicles. When viewed this way, the similarities between guys' and dolls' private parts is obvious and has drawn comments since ancient Greek times.

But there's a whole lot more overlap than you might suspect. Women aren't the only ones who have a clitoris. Men do, too.

To fully understand this, it helps to know some things about our naughty bits. In women, the clit is a much larger organ than it generally gets credit for being. That little bit of ultrasensitive tissue that is the target of so much attention is merely the tip of the iceberg. The visible part that is touched and tasted is the crown, typically 0.25 to 0.75 of an inch in length. Hidden from view is the other 2.75 to 5 inches of the structure! The entire thing is shaped like a Y, with the visible crown leading to the section called the body, which then splits into two legs that hug the urethra and vagina canal.

This 3- to 5.75-inch structure is made of two sandwiched strips of *corpora cavernosa*, a tissue that engorges with blood and stiffens when its owner is aroused.

Turning to the penis, we see that its insides are made up of two kinds of tissue. The thin *corpus spongiosum* runs along the underside of the shaft, enveloping the urethra, and accounts for all of the head. This tissue plays a minor role in erections, since a hard-on is due mostly to the two sandwiched strips of *corpora cavernosa*, which comprise the bulk of the shaft. These taper off internally right as they reach the *spongiosum* dickhead.

As in women, a man's *cavernosa* soaks up blood and becomes erect when sexually excited. As in women, the *cavernosa* is shaped like a Y with three parts — crown, body, legs. In the case of men, the body accounts for more of the structure, and the legs are relatively stubby. On average, the male *cavernosa* is typically longer and thicker (which makes sense, since men as a group are bigger than women), and — unlike women — the majority of it is visible.

So here's what we have: the same tissue forming the same structure in the same place. In other words, it's the same thing.

A penis is really a clitoris that's been pulled mostly out of the body and grafted on top of a much smaller piece of *spongiosum* containing the urethra. ⚲

As much as I'd like to be known as the person who first realized that men have clits, the credit goes to psychologist-anatomist-sexologist Josephine Lowndes Sevely for first making this explicit in 1987. Science writer Catherine Blackledge expanded on it in 2004.

02
OUT OF EVERY 100 PEOPLE, TEN WEREN'T FATHERED BY THE MAN THEY BELIEVE IS DAD

Geneticists, disease researchers, and evolutionary psychologists have known it for a while, but the statistic hasn't gotten much air outside of the ivory tower. Consistently, they find that one in ten of us wasn't fathered by the man we think is our biological dad.

Naturally, adoptees and stepchildren realize their paternal situation. What we're talking about here is people who have taken it as a given, for their entire lives, that dear old Dad is the one who contributed his sperm to the process. Even Dad himself may be under this impression. And Mom, knowing it's not a sure thing, just keeps quiet.

Genetic testing companies report that almost one-third of the time, samples sent to them show that the man is not father to the child. But these companies are used when there's a court order in a paternity suit or when a man gets suspicious because his kid looks a lot like his best friend or his wife's coworker. So we shouldn't be surprised that the non-paternity rate for these tests hovers around 30 percent.

The shocker comes when we look at the numbers for accidental discoveries, those that occur when paternity isn't thought to be an issue. Sometimes this happens on an individual basis; other times, due to large-scale studies of blood types, disease susceptibility, kinship, and other fields of medical and scientific investigation.

Dr. Caoilfhionn Gallagher of the University College Dublin gives an example of the former:

The paradigmatic situation is that three people come to a hospital together, a husband, wife and their child who they fear has cystic fibrosis. If the child has the incurable disease she must have received two copies of the CF gene, one from each parent. Tests at the hospital confirm the family's worst fears — she has the disease — but also reveal something unexpected. The child's mother carries one of the culprit genes, but the father's DNA shows no such sign, which means he is not the carrier and therefore cannot possibly be her biological father.

The latter type of discovery occurred in *the* classic case from the early 1970s. Scientists were eyeballing blood types in the British town of West Isleworth, taking the red stuff from entire families. They realized, to their dismay, that fully 30 percent of the children had blood types which proved that they couldn't possibly be biologically related to their "fathers." The true rate of illegitimacy was still higher, though, because even some fathers and bastards would have matching blood types due to coincidence. The researchers estimated that the true rate was around 50 percent.

Other studies have found a 20-30 percent rate in Liverpool, 10 percent in rural Michigan, and 2.3 percent among native Hawaiians. The overall figure of 10 percent is actually an average estimate based on many studies taking place in sundry regions over the course of decades. In his book *Sperm Wars: The Science of Sex*, biologist Robin Baker, PhD, summarizes the stats:

Actual figures range from 1 percent in high-status areas of the United States and Switzerland, to 5 to 6 percent for moderate-status males in the United States and Great Britain, to 10 to 30 percent for lower-status males in the United States, Great Britain and France.

The prestigious medical journal *The Lancet* concurs: "The true frequency of non-paternity is not known, but published reports suggest an incidence from as low as 1% per generation up to about 30% in the population."

The research shows that the lower a purported father's socioeconomic status, the more likely his wife got someone else to father the child. From a Darwinian standpoint this makes perfect sense, since she wants her offspring to have the highest-caliber DNA, which may not come from the stiff she settled for at the altar.

This knowledge should make Father's Day a much more interesting, and introspective, holiday.

03
HARDCORE SEXUAL IMAGERY
IS AS OLD AS THE HUMAN RACE

Sometimes it's directly spoken, and sometimes it floats unsaid in the background — the idea that visual hardcore pornography is something unique to our decadent, modern society. Only in the past few decades have graphic representations of sex sprung into existence, according to this naïve belief. These things would send our innocent forebears into cardiac arrest. Whether you dig porn or whether you think it's filth that's rotting our sick society (or both), there's a tendency to view it in an ahistorical vacuum. Visuals depicting full-penetration sex acts, engorged penises, and/or spread-open labia made their appearance in the mists of prehistory and have never gone away.

Cave and rock drawings around the world limn the real or imagined doings of our ancestors. The famous rock art at Fezzan in the Sahara Desert, dated to about 5000 BC, shows manimal hybrids with enormous schlongs, some almost as big as the rest of their bodies. In some scenes, they're penetrating spread women. Caves in Italy, Spain, Russia, India, and Meso-potamia also portray Neandertals boffing. A drawing of doggie-style sex in a French cave has been dated to 40,000 BC.

China has contributed a considerable amount of sex imagery to the world, including coins showing gods and goddesses screwing, minted during the Han Dynasty (206 BC – 220 AD), and the illustrated "pillow books" from the nineteenth century.

The ancient Greeks drenched their vases, plates, goblets, and other objects with a litany of anal, oral, and vaginal sex — two men doing a woman or a third guy from both ends, young mixed-sex couples, old men and young boys, men with animals, women loving women, satyrs fucking nubile flesh.

When the ruins of Pompeii were excavated, Victorian archaeologists must've gone white when confronted with frescos showing the same things that fascinated the Greeks, only these were rendered in a realistic style using full color. When the relics were put on display in Naples National Museum, not all of them made the cut. The dildos, fornicating frescoes, some statues (like the one of a satyr humping a goat), and other explicit works were kept in a secret room that was sealed off from the public for around 200 years.

The Egyptians were no prudes, either. Pharaohs were sometimes rendered with rock-hard stiffies, and the Ani Papyrus shows us how they got that way: A woman kneels before the pharaoh, giving him a blowjob in a ritual known as the animation of the phallus (in the porn industry, she'd be called a fluffer). Other artwork shows women, bent at the waist, being penetrated by guys with impossibly long, thin dicks.

Engravings for bawdy Medieval literary masterpieces such as *The Decameron* and *Gargantua and Pantagruel* could still make people blush. The same can be said of the hardcore etchings and engravings that flourished during the Renaissance and into the 1700s. A series of etchings accompanying a Dutch edition of de Sade's *Juliette* may still be unrivaled for the sheer inventiveness and scope of the clusterfucks they depict.

If you thought that sexual photography started with *Playboy* and cheesecake in the 1950s, you're off by a full century. Daguerreotypes of naked women started showing up in the late 1840s in France, not long after the process was unveiled in 1839. At first, the images were the exclusive playthings of the rich, but the photographers quickly realized that a huge market existed for their work, triggering a tsunami of mass-produced images starting in the 1850s.

Though many of the women in these shots appear demure and adopt poses from classical art, the nudity is fully frontal. Some of these old photos dispense with coyness altogether — what we would today call a split-beaver shot appeared in 1851. That same time period saw photos of women giving each other enemas. Pictures of ladies flagellating each other arrived only a few years later, as did images of women being penetrated by stiff cocks. Although rare at first, these pictures of sex and genitals became more common as the decades progressed. One of the most popular of the erotic photos carried by soldiers during the US Civil War was a shot of a woman whole-heartedly spreading her legs right at the camera.

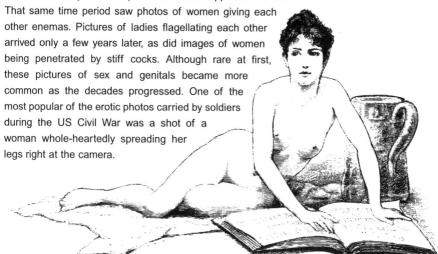

History professor Jonathan Coopersmith writes: "The scale of production of photographs, postcards and slides was enormous: an 1874 police raid on London pornographer Henry Haylor found 130,248 obscene photos and 5,000 obscene slides."

Photos of nekkid dudes took longer to reach the masses. Shutterbugs were snapping pics of nude men in the 1850s for painters to use as reference, but it wasn't until close to 1900 that these photos "for the use of artists" (nudge, wink) were sold on a much wider basis.

The first porn film was created in 1896, not long after the invention of motion picture technology as we know it. "Stag films" soon became an underground sensation, with informal gatherings of men watching these hardcore sex flicks that had been shot on 8 mm or 16 mm film. The Kinsey Institute's collection holds 1,697 of these nuggets going all the way back to 1913.

Still photography and film continued to be used for the creation of one-handed material during the entire twentieth century, finally going mainstream with *Playboy*, *Penthouse*, *I Am Curious (Yellow)*, *Deep Throat*, the VCR, and the Internet.

A menace to society? Hardcore sex imagery has been around continuously since some troglodyte first scribbled on a cave wall, yet somehow the human race survives. ⌯

04
SHAKESPEARE'S WORKS ARE LOADED WITH SEXUAL JOKES AND TERMS

For almost all of us, our only exposure to Shakespeare's writings came in high school and college. Which means that we probably never heard that his work is rife with sexual puns and imagery, since teachers and professors aren't too quick to mention this aspect of the Bard. Besides a general taboo against sexual matters (not to mention fear of being censured by school boards or faculty committees, or even sued by bluenose students), the whitewashing is done for the same reason it's always done — to protect reputations, in this case Shakespeare's. Instructors are trying as hard as they can to convince impressionable minds of Shakespeare's genius and importance, so it wouldn't do to tell them that the greatest writer in the English language played around with "fuck," "cunt," and "prick." Haven't we been told that only people with no imagination and poor vocabularies resort to such foul language?

Shakespeare was enamored with vaginas. In his groundbreaking work, *Shakespeare's Bawdy*, mainstream scholar Eric Partridge lists 68 terms that the Bard used in both direct references and double *entendres*: "bird's nest," "box unseen," "crack," "flower," "forfended place," "hole," "nest of spicery," "Netherlands," "O," "Pillicock-hill," "salmon's tail," "secret parts," "Venus' glove," "withered pear," "wound," and dozens more.

Penises didn't rank quite as high in Shakespeare's mind, but Partridge still finds 45 dick euphemisms in the works, including "bugle," "dart of love," "instrument," "little finger," "loins," "pizzle," "potato-finger," "thorn," and "tool."

Some of Shakespeare's indecencies are lost on us moderns. But when you learn that "to die" also meant to orgasm, you get the joke in *Much Ado About Nothing* when Benedick tells his ladylove: "I will live in thy heart, die in thy lap, and be buried in thy eyes."

Sometimes it's not that subtle, like when Mercutio tells the Nurse in *Romeo and Juliet* that "the bawdy hand of the dial is now upon the prick of noon." Besides the overt imagery of a "bawdy hand" on a "prick," Shakespeare's also making a sly reference to the hands of a clock being straight up at 12 o'clock.

William even invented a highly visual slang term for sex that's still in use. In *Othello*, Iago informs Brabantio: "I am one, sir, that comes to tell you your daughter and the Moor [i.e., Othello] are now making the beast with two backs."

The Bard never directly used the word "fuck," but he did pun on it. In *The Merry Wives of Windsor*, as Sir Hugh Evans tries to teach Latin, a bizarre speech impediment involving the letter "V" makes him talk about the "focative" case. This is immediately followed by him mentioning the Latin word *caret* (a homophone of "carrot"), which a female character assures us is "a good root."

The word also makes a disguised appearance in *Henry V*. Act 3, scene 4 is delivered almost entirely in French, and its sole purpose is to lead up to a linguistic sex joke. Katherine asks Alice to tell her the English words for various body parts (elbow, nails, etc.). Toward the end, she wants to know how to say "*le pied et la robe*" ("foot and dress") in English. Alice tells her that they're "foot" and "coun" (she means "gown" but badly mispronounces it). Katherine mistakes this for the French words meaning "fuck" (*foutre*) and "cunt" (*con*), leading her to screech — in French — that those words "should not be used by a lady-in-waiting."

"Cunt" makes another appearance — punned in the word "country" — in this exchange from *Hamlet*, in which Ophelia thinks the Dane is aiming to get some nookie:

Hamlet: **Lady, shall I lie in your lap?**
Ophelia: **No, my lord.**
Hamlet: **I mean, my head upon your lap?**
Ophelia: **Ay, my lord.**
Hamlet: **Do you think I meant country matters?**

Perhaps funniest of all, we have the scene from *Twelfth Night* in which Malvolio reads a letter and thinks the handwriting is that of Olivia, the object of his love. He exclaims that "these be her very C's, her U's and her T's and thus makes she her great P's." Apparently, the word "and" should be pronounced lazily, so that it sounds like "N" and completes the word. We even get a bonus excretory joke when Malvolio says that Olivia urinates ("P's") profusely with her cunt.

That Shakespeare! You can't turn your back on him for a minute. 🗘

05
BARBIE IS BASED ON A GERMAN SEX DOLL

The world's most famous doll — that twentieth century icon, Barbie — didn't just appear full-blown from the mind of her creator, Ruth Handler. Barbie's inspiration, her immediate predecessor, is an overtly sexual hottie named Lilli.

Lilli started out as a cartoon character drawn by Reinhard Beuthien for the Hamburg tabloid newspaper *Bild-Zeitung*. This blonde, curvy bombshell who pursued rich men first appeared in ink in 1952. Three years later, she became a plastic doll in Germany. The definitive history *Forever Barbie* reveals: "The doll, sold principally in tobacco shops, was marketed as a sort of three-dimensional pinup. ... Lilli was never intended for children: She was a pornographic caricature, a gag gift for men..." Mattel engineer Jack Ryan once called Lilli a "hooker or an actress between performances."

Ruth Handler — she and her husband were cofounders of Mattel — wanted to create a three-dimensional, plastic, grown-up doll for girls, but the company's all-male board nixed the idea. While in Europe, she happened upon the vixenish Lilli and knew that she had discovered the literal prototype for her unrealized doll. The original Barbies were deliberately based on the German mantrap (Barb's head, in fact, was cast from Lilli's with a few minor tweaks).

When the first Barbie appeared in 1959, it was as if Lilli had been cloned. They had the same puckered, fire-engine red lips, same arched eyebrows, same almond-shaped eyes glancing sidelong, same golden hair pulled into a ponytail, same height (11.5 inches), same pencil-thin legs, same wasp waist with pneumatic breasts above and child-bearing hips below.

Barbie's similarity to her slutty forerunner didn't go unnoticed. During pre-release market testing, mothers complained about Barbie's sex vibe, saying things like, "I don't like that influence on my little girl," and, "They could be a cute decoration for a man's bar." Sears — purveyors of the almighty Christmas "Wishbook" — refused to carry her at first. Nonetheless, Barbie instantly became a huge hit with girls, and Mattel spent the early years making her less of a tart. Now, every second of the day, two Barbies are sold. Lilli must be green with envy.

06
FETUSES MASTURBATE

In 1996, two ob-gyns in Italy published a letter in the *American Journal of Obstetrics and Gynecology*. The heart of the matter was this:

We recently observed a female fetus at 32 weeks' gestation touching the vulva with the fingers of the right hand. The caressing movements were centered primarily on the region of the clitoris. Movements stopped after 30 to 40 seconds and started again after a few minutes. Furthermore, these slight touches were repeated and were associated with short, rapid movements of pelvis and legs. After another break, in addition to this behavior, the fetus contracted the muscles of the trunk and limbs, and then clonicotonic movements [ie, prolonged spasms] of the whole body followed. Finally, she relaxed and rested.

We observed this behavior for about 20 minutes. The mother was an active and interested witness, conversing with observers about her child's experience.

They drew the conclusion: "The female sexual response is separate from reproductive functions and doesn't need a full sexual maturity to be explicit."

The Italians also noted: "Evidence of male fetuses' excitement reflex in utero, such as erection or 'masturbation' movements, has been previously reported." This is a reference to a letter by Dr. Israel Meizner, published in the *Journal of Ultrasound Medicine*, in which the fetal ultrasound expert spies on an unborn boy bopping his baloney.

In 1995, the British science series *Equinox* achieved a first when it broadcast ultrasound footage of another male fetus playing with himself.

Sadly, a literature search shows that no one has yet published a full-fledged study of zesty zygotes, but the field is ripe for study. Dean Edell, MD (a/k/a, "America's doctor") has written: "It is common during second trimester ultrasonography examinations to see the fetus touch itself repeatedly and rhythmically on the genitalia, offering fairly compelling proof that masturbation is rooted not in sin but in biology."

07
SOME LEGAL, READILY AVAILABLE SUBSTANCES CAN GET USERS HIGH

As hard as it is to believe, the Drug Warriors have actually neglected to outlaw some common substances that can alter consciousness in a pleasurable way. As you might guess, the high from some of these goodies often leaves much to be desired when compared with their *verboten* cousins, but people who are desperate, gun-shy, or out to experience everything they can often indulge in them. We draw attention to these under-the-radar substances not to suggest that you try them but to thumb our noses at the arrogant thugs who tell us what we can and can't put into our bodies.

Nutmeg. Ingesting the proper dose of this spice can lead to a day and a half of pleasant experiences. Or not. Users seem to agree that it takes one or two hours for the first stage to hit, which may be a buzz, mellowness, or grogginess. After another few hours reality

seems altered — nutmeggers experience visuals, mild hallucinations, a dreamlike state, zoning out, "lucid day-dreaming," maybe even bliss. For the entire next day, trippers are languid and drowsy. But some people don't get much out of it except for feeling dizzy and tired, while others have bad reactions including racing heart and bazooka-barfing. One dissatisfied customer on the Web ended his experience with: "I'd seriously rather eat shit."

Catnip. Not just for felines anymore, catnip reportedly will give you a low-grade pot-like buzz if smoked. Experienced puffers say it works better when mixed with tobacco.

Lettuce opium. All permutations of lettuce contain an opium-like alkaloid called lactucarium. For decades, people in search of a cheap legal high have liquefied whole heads of lettuce, letting the juice evaporate and gel into a gummy substance, which is then toked. As catnip is to weed, so lettuce opium is to poppy opium — a pale imitation but better than nothing.

Cough syrup. "Doing 'tussin" — chugging cough syrup, such as Robotussin, containing the suppressant DXM — is quite popular with the legal high crowd, since you can get the goods at any drug store, and who's going to question a bottle of it in your medicine cabinet? Like nutmeg, user reports range from practically achieving nirvana to being dragged through the slimiest pits of hell. The high number of negative reports from users is a red flag.

Poppies. Going into a flower shop or an arts-and-crafts store to score might seem strange, but many of these places sell poppies. As in opium poppies. Growing the flowers is legal for the most part, but taking any steps to harvest the opium isn't. Still, the pods can be ground up and brewed to make poppy tea, while a small number of people steep the seeds in lemon juice and drink the resulting grog. Not that this is a good idea, since addiction to opiates is a hellish nightmare, but it can be done.

Nitrous oxide. Next to the flower shop with poppies is a kitchen supply or gourmet food store (who knew the mall was such a den of inequity?). They carry nitrous oxide chargers, the stuff that puts the fluff into homemade whipped cream. On the street, these palm-sized tubes are called "whippits," and the nitrous — "laughing gas" from the dentist's office — can be discharged into a heavy-duty balloon or a gadget known as a cracker, from whence it is inhaled. (Trying to suck the gas straight from the charger results in damaging skin freeze.)

Solvents and jimsonweed. As a friend of mine has said, if you're thinking of huffing solvents or ingesting jimsonweed, you might as well just bash yourself in the head with a hammer. It produces the same basic "altered state" with about as much damage.

Finally, I'd be remiss if I didn't give at least a passing mention to those three super-legal drugs: caffeine, tobacco, and alcohol.… ⧜

08
A DEA JUDGE RULED THAT POT IS MEDICALLY BENEFICIAL

For two years starting in 1986, the Drug Enforcement Administration held historic hearings aimed at the possible rescheduling of marijuana, which was and still is laughably designated as a Schedule I drug, along with heroin, ecstasy, LSD, and mescaline.

According to federal law, a substance is put on Schedule I — the most stringent level of control — if it "has a high potential for abuse," "has no currently accepted medical use in treatment in the United States," and there exists "a lack of accepted safety for use of the drug or other substance under medical supervision." Since marijuana is a nontoxic, nonaddictive plant with a millennia-long history of health uses, it utterly fails to deserve a spot in Schedule I.

Under the Controlled Substances Act, parties can petition for rescheduling of any substance, and the DEA must formally consider the request. The National Organization for the Reform of Marijuana Law and thirteen individuals with various medical conditions went through the steps to move weed to the slightly less draconian Schedule II, where it would still be considered a generally evil, destructive substance but could be more widely used for medical purposes. It took three lawsuits and two direct court orders to force the DEA to hold hearings.

During the proceedings, patients and family members testified about pot's near-miraculous ability to take away the overwhelming nausea caused by chemotherapy, its deflating of the internal eye pressure that causes glaucoma, its merciful relief of chronic pain and itching, and the way it tames spasticity. The mother of a teenager who died of testicular cancer told how chemo would make him violently vomit and dry heave for days, but if he smoked chronic before and after therapy, he'd eat dinner with the family that very night. She said: "It was clear to us that marijuana was the safest, most benign drug he received during the course of his battle against cancer."

Bunches of doctors — including oncologists, ophthalmologists, psychiatrists, and alternative health guru Andrew Weil, MD — testified on the benefits of *Cannabis sativa*. Cancer doctor Ivan Silverberg, MD, declared under oath: "It [using marijuana] has simply become a standard routine, accepted as part of the practice of Oncology."

Seventy-two articles from medical journals were placed into the record. NORML entered into evidence a list of 33 states that passed statutes recognizing pot's medicinal value.

On the side of the DEA and other Drug Warriors, a number of heartless doctors repeated the prohibitionist mantras that pot is no more effective than synthetic THC (to which patients who've tried both unanimously say bullshit) and that there's not enough scientific evidence to support pot's efficacy (never mind the fact that its illegality makes it almost impossible to scientifically study).

In the end, the DEA's administrative judge ruled in favor of sanity and compassion: He decreed that marijuana should be moved to Schedule II, where it can be widely used under a doc's care. In his ruling, Judge Francis L. Young wrote:

Marijuana, in its natural form, is one of the safest therapeutically active substances known to man. By any measure of rational analysis marijuana can be

safely used within a supervised routine of medical care. ...

The evidence in this record clearly shows that marijuana has been accepted as capable of relieving the distress of great numbers of very ill people, and doing so with safety under medical supervision. It would be unreasoning, arbitrary and capricious for [the] DEA to continue to stand between those sufferers and the benefit of this substance in light of the evidence on record.

Such enlightened thinking could not be allowed to stand, of course. The head of the DEA simply rejected his own judge's ruling, and there the matter ended. ⌗

09
EACH MONTH, NEW WARNINGS ARE ADDED TO THE LABELS OF 40 DRUGS

Every month, the FDA posts a list of all drugs that have had "safety labeling changes to the contraindications, boxed warning, warnings, precautions, or adverse reactions sections." In other words, these drugs are more dangerous, and dangerous in different ways, than their makers knew (or admitted) when they were declared fit for the American public. Now the pharmaceutical corporations have been forced to tell us about more dangers, problems, contraindications, and side effects regarding the products that millions of people are already using.

During 2003 and the first five months of 2004, an average of 40 drugs received revised labels each month, for an average of almost two every business day. May 2004 produced the highest number, a bumper crop of 65 new warnings, while March of that year came in second, with 59.

Even the massively marketed drugs that have become household names get hit. Clarinex, Effexor, Flonase, Flovent, Nasacort, Ritalin, Xanax, Zithromax, and Zyprexa are among those with new warnings during the time period.

Suprax (cefixime) — used to treat bacterial infections — now is admitted to cause angioedema (swelling of the heart), facial edema, hepatitis, jaundice, acute renal failure, seizures, and toxic epidermal necrolysis (death of the flesh). The new label tells us: "Anaphylactic/anaphylactoid reactions (including shock and fatalities) have been reported with the use of cefixime."

Vioxx, which is supposed to treat pain, now warns that it can cause: "Migraine with or without aura." The heavily advertised allergy medication Zyrtec has been admitted to rarely cause blocking of the liver's bile ducts, swelling of the kidneys, destruction of red blood cells, hepatitis, involuntary facial movements, severely low blood pressure, stillbirth, and "aggressive reaction and convulsions."

The "healing purple pill" Nexium had bad news after it was released, with some patients developing fatal cases of skin necrosis, not to mention nonfatal cases of pancreatitis and Stevens-Johnson syndrome. Invanz added hallucinations to its label when "post-marketing experience" showed that some patients started tripping after being injected with the antibacterial drug. Similarly, after the high blood pressure medication Atacand was already in use, it was reported to be deforming and killing fetuses. Merck had to add a new box warning to

AquaMEPHYTON — its Vitamin K1 solution — when it began killing people, especially when given intravenously.

In one of the longest lags between a drug's introduction and a new warning, Demerol, a widely used pain reliever, got a new warning in February 2003: It passes straight into mother's milk, so suckling babies are ingesting this powerful, addictive narcotic if their mommies take it. Demerol was introduced in the 1930s. It took 70 years to discover that Demmies pass unaltered into breast milk?

Perhaps most significant, in spring 2004, after years of mounting evidence, six major antidepressants (Paxil, Wellbutrin, Effexor, Serzone, Celexa, Lexapro) finally received label changes warning doctors and shrinks to monitor patients for increased suicidality when starting, increasing, or decreasing any of the drugs.

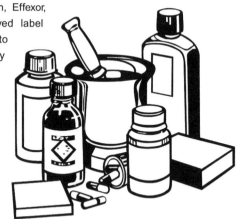

One of the scariest label changes happened to Pletal (cilostazol) Tablets, which "are used to treat intermittent claud-ication, a condition in which a person experiences pain or discomfort when walking that stops with rest." The "adverse reactions" portion of the label was updated in February 2004 to include the following litany of horrors that have shown up now that the public is taking the drug:

Postmarketing Experience

The following adverse events have been reported worldwide since the launch of Pletal in the US: pain, chest pain, hot flushes, cerebral hemorrhage, angina pectoris, hypotension, hepatic dysfunction/abnormal liver function tests, jaundice, vomiting, thrombocytopenia, leukopenia, bleeding tendency, paresthesia, hyperglycemia, pulmonary hemorrhage, interstitial pneumonia, pruritus, skin eruptions including Stevens-Johnson syndrome, rash, increase BUN, and hematuria.

The following adverse events occurred outside the US prior to marketing of Pletal in the US: pulmonary hemorrhage and Stevens-Johnson syndrome.

Did you catch that last sentence? Massive bleeding of the heart and an excruciating, disfiguring skin reaction that sometimes kills you showed up *before* the drug was offered in the US. But it was sold to Americans anyway. Thanks for the warning. ▯

10
SUVS ARE OVER 3 TIMES MORE LIKELY THAN CARS TO KILL PEDESTRIANS WHO ARE STRUCK

If you're one of the 86,500 pedestrians who get smashed by motor vehicles each year in the US, better hope it's not a "light truck" — an SUV, pickup truck, or van — that knocks you flying. These vehicles are 3.4 times as likely to kill you as a car.

In a study published in the journal *Injury Prevention*, researchers from the Universities of Washington and Virginia crunched fatality stats from six US cities, including Chicago and Seattle, which had been collected by the National Highway Safety Administration.

When they broke down the numbers by type of vehicle, sure enough, the goliaths of the road are more likely to leave corpses in their wake. They're not just twice as lethal, or even three times as lethal. They're almost three-and-a-half times as deadly. And when it comes to serious injuries that don't result in a funeral, the "light truck" rate is three times that of cars.

The numbers for the study were collected from 1994 to 1998. In the years since, SUVs and pickups have become much bigger and more powerful as consumers compete for higher status and intimidation factor. It stands to reason, then, that the lethality of these quasi-tanks has only increased. ▯

11
ARISTOTLE SET BACK SCIENCE FOR AROUND 2,000 YEARS

Aristotle may have been a genius when it came to philosophy — especially logic — but he didn't know squat about science. Sure, we can't excel in every field we try our hand in, but Aristotle's massive errors aren't just a personal embarrassment to him — they directly hampered scientific progress for 1,800 to 2,000 years.

The problem is that from the time he was alive (the fourth century BC) until the Enlightenment, when Aristotle said something, that was the end of the argument. Isaac Asimov notes, perhaps with a tinge of jealousy: "No matter who disagreed with them, even other philosophers, Aristotle's ideas — whether right or wrong — usually won out." Chemist John Appeldoorn writes that "Aristotle's teachings were unquestioned. After eighteen centuries, universities accepted them as if they had been written in stone."

For example, Aristotle didn't believe that plants were divided into male and female sexes, so there the matter stood for two millennia, until botanists stated the obvious in the 1700s.

He was also wrong about inertia, and again the world had to wait — this time for Galileo, followed by Newton — to speak the truth that objects in motion stay in motion, while objects at rest stay at rest, unless acted upon by outside forces.

Like most Greeks, Aristotle championed the view that the Sun and planets revolved around the Earth. Copernicus (in the early 1500s) and Galileo (100 years later) had to risk their reputations and their lives to put the kibosh on that nonsense.

He further surmised that outer space was made up of 54 spheres and that there were only seven heavenly bodies, which were fixed and unchanging. This meant, for one thing, that comets had to be in Earth's atmosphere. Only in 1577 was this notion put out to pasture. Over the next 50 years, belief in the heavenly spheres faded.

Aristotle declared that heavier objects fall faster than lighter ones, an error that could've been exposed with simple experiments. It wasn't until 1,900 years later that Galileo dropped objects off the Tower of Pisa, proving that all things obey gravity at the same rate. By that time, Galileo already had been kicked out of the University of Pisa for daring to question Aristotle's theory.

Some Greeks, including Democritus and Hippocrates, surmised that the brain was the seat of thought, intelligence, and emotion. Tish-tosh, said Aristotle, it's the heart — and that became the accepted wisdom. Aristotle wrote: "The brain is an organ of minor importance, perhaps necessary to cool the blood." Because Greek physicians primarily held brain-centered views, that remained a strong undercurrent, yet Aristotle's heart view dominated until the 1500s.

A fellow Greek philosopher, Democritus, postulated that the physical world was made up of tiny pieces of matter, which he called atoms. But Aristotle pooh-poohed this ridiculous notion, causing it to languish in obscurity until the second half of the 1600s, when scientists began to resurrect it. It wasn't until the first years of the 1800s that the existence of atoms was universally accepted.

Who knows how much further science would've progressed if Aristotle had stuck to syllogisms?

12
NATIVE AMERICANS WERE KEPT AS SLAVES

When we think of US slavery, we think of Africans being forced to work in the fields and the master's house. Some mainstream sources will give a nod to enslaved white people, although they're almost always labeled with the euphemism "indentured servants." But you'll never hear about Native American slaves. Not because they didn't exist, but because they've been thrown into history's dustbin.

Columbus wasted little time before enslaving the native people on Hispaniola. The Spanish proceeded to make slaves out of the indigenous people all over the Caribbean, Latin America, Florida, and what is now the Southwestern US. The French did the same thing in Canada and Louisiana, as did the Portuguese in Brazil. From the early 1600s, the British were the primary enslavers of Indians in what we now call the Eastern US.

Native Americans were put to the lash in most colonies and territories east of the Mississippi River — including New York, Massachusetts, Rhode Island, Pennsylvania, Virginia, the Carolinas, Georgia — as well as the areas that were or became Arkansas, Kansas, Nebraska, Utah, New Mexico, and Arizona. A small number of Native Americans were taken from the West Indies to the American colonies, but by far most of the traffic was the reverse, with the mainland supplying the islands with Indian slaves to handle crops such as sugar.

How did the European colonists get their hands on Indian slaves? Many were captured directly during wars between Europeans and Native Americans. In some cases, Indians sold their children into slavery. In a third route, perhaps accounting for most slaves, Indian tribes sold their captives to the palefaces. As in Africa, slaves largely were not captured by Europeans but were snared by neighboring tribes, who then sold them to the white men. At first, Native Americans simply sold their prisoners of war, but tribes quickly started raiding other tribes for the sole purpose of snatching human chattel for the settlers.

The various European groups started using Indian slaves almost as soon as they set up settlements. The Yamasee war almost, but not quite, eliminated the practice in 1715 in the Southeast. The Spanish made slaves out of Indians in southern Mexico, continuing the practice as they pushed north of the Rio Grande, forcing their captives to work primarily in mines and as household servants. The practice slowed down a few years after the US wrested the Southwest from Mexico in 1848, but it definitely didn't stop. Even the Civil War didn't halt the practice. Immediately after the War Between the States, though, Congress took up the issue of Indian slavery in the Southwest, eventually directing William T. Sherman to liberate the captive Native Americans. (Although this effectively ended the slave trade, the practice of slaveholding didn't completely stop; a rancher in Arizona is known to have kept a female Apache, captured when she was fourteen, into the 1930s.)

In his scholarly book *The Indian Slave Trade*, history professor Alan Gallay notes: "Most Indian slaves were women and children, whereas the majority of African slaves were adult males." Native Americans generally didn't make ideal slaves for various reasons. One of the main "problems" was that they could more easily fly the coop and rejoin their tribe or at least a friendly tribe. They also had a hard time resisting all those funky European diseases. Because of this, their numbers never came close to those of African slaves.

How many Native Americans were enslaved will never be known, so we have only very rough estimates. This trade wasn't documented nearly to the extent of its African counterpart, and most of the records that were created haven't survived. Professor Gallay has assembled what pieces remain to come up with a probable range of Indians who were enslaved by the British in the Southeast up to 1715: no less than 25,000 to 32,200, and no more than 51,000. In the seriously obscure book *Indian Slave Trade in the Southwest*, L.R. Bailey cites 6,000 slaves in the territory of New Mexico when the Civil War broke out.

So we're up to 31,000 to 57,000 without including any of New England, New York, the Southeast *after* 1715, antebellum New Mexico, the rest of the Southwest, the Plains states, or the Indians enslaved by Spaniards in Florida and the French in Louisiana. And that's only part of the hemispheric picture; native peoples enslaved in Canada, Central and South America, and the Caribbean islands obviously would add lots of misery to the total. ▢

13
GEORGE WASHINGTON EMBEZZLED GOVERNMENT FUNDS

We typically imagine George Washington to be as pure as driven snow, a demigod who won the Revolutionary War, then assumed the mantle of President to flawlessly lead a fledgling country.

The reality is vastly different. Besides being borderline incompetent on the battlefield (during the first four years of the Revolution, he lost *every* major engagement), the man who could not tell a lie started the tradition of presidential corruption.

The whistle was blown by the Clerk of Congress — writing under the *nom de plume* "A Calm Observer" — in the *Philadelphia Aurora*, a muckraking anti-federalist newspaper founded, edited, and published by Benjamin Franklin's grandson. In 1795, the *Aurora* published the Clerk's detailed breakdown of how much loot Washington had taken from the Treasury beyond his Constitutionally-sanctioned $25,000 annual salary.

According to the paperwork seen by the Clerk, the Father of Our Country started out honest, drawing exactly his salary of $25K during year one. But over the course of the second year, he took $30,150, thus embezzling $5,150. In his third year, perhaps suffering a pang on conscience, GW took a little less than his entitlement: $24,000. He made up for it during his fourth year, though, by filching an extra grand.

In February 1793, as Washington's second term was about to begin, Congress passed an act calling for the President to be paid on a quarterly basis (i.e., $6,250 every three months). But during the first quarter of his second term, Washington took $11,000 from the Treasury.

At this point, the Clerk of Congress must've lost access to the smoking guns, since he wonders whether the graft continued after Q1 of the second term. He presciently asks: "If the precedent which this donation from the treasury furnishes, were to be allowed in favour of other public officers, how many hundred thousand dollars per annum would thus be lawlessly taken from the public treasury and saddled upon the people?" 🖵

14
THE DECLARATION OF INDEPENDENCE CONTAINS
A RACIALLY DEROGATORY REMARK

Wouldn't it be shocking to find that one of the United States' two most important founding documents contains a racial slur? That it denigrates lazy "darkies"? Or conniving "slant-eyes"? Or bloodthirsty "savages"?

Those first two examples aren't in the US Declaration of Independence, but the last one is. When airing their grievances against King George III, the Founders wrote:

He has excited domestic insurrections amongst us, and has endeavoured to bring on the inhabitants of our frontiers, the merciless Indian Savages, whose known rule of warfare, is an undistinguished destruction of all ages, sexes and conditions.

Of course, the truth of the matter is that some Native Americans did indeed massacre settlers. But some settlers, not to mention military troops, were also slaughtering Indians. And just who was encroaching on whom?

Now, I'm not saying we should change the Declaration; I'm opposed to revising the past, and that goes double for such a momentous document. But if I were a Native American, knowing that my country's first landmark document slurs my people wouldn't sit well.

On a related note, California's Constitution (the second version, from 1879, which is still in force) contained horrible slurs and measures against Chinese people. It specified that no private or public employer may hire Chinese, that Chinese should be thrown out of cities and towns, and that the state should bar them from entering. A particularly vicious clause called on the legislature to take action against the "burdens and evils arising from the presence of aliens who are or may become vagrants, paupers, mendicants, criminals, or invalids afflicted with contagious or infectious diseases, and from aliens otherwise dangerous or detrimental to the well-being or peace of the State." Those racist sections were soon declared unconstitutional by the courts and were struck from the constitution. ⌗

15
JAMES AUDUBON KILLED ALL THE BIRDS HE PAINTED

One of America's great naturalists, John James Audubon painted highly realistic portraits of practically every type of bird in North America. The self-taught artist's resulting four-volume collection of life-size paintings, *The Birds of America* (1827–38), is regarded as both an artistic and an ornithological masterpiece, and reproductions of his work are still brightening walls around the world.

But exactly how Audubon was able to capture our feathered friends' likenesses so completely is usually glossed over. The *Encyclopedia Britannica* fails to even broach the subject. The Audubon Society's page on their namesake mentions that he loved to hunt, but the connection is never explicitly made.

Audubon shot all the birds he painted. He then used wires to pose the corpses of these hawks, falcons, partridges, sparrows, woodpeckers, and other winged creatures before putting brush to canvas. In one diary entry, he writes about sneaking up on a large group of sleeping pelicans and blasting two of them before his gun jammed and the awakened survivors took off (he was disappointed that he didn't get to kill them all). And when hunting snoozing avians in the wild was too much trouble, he resorted to other methods. He once bought a caged eagle, killed it, then captured its likeness.

One of Audubon's biographers, Duff Hart-Davis, reveals: "The rarer the bird, the more eagerly he pursued it, never apparently worrying that by killing it he might hasten the extinction of its kind."

Over 1,000 individual birds appear in Audubon's paintings, but we know that the body count is much higher. He didn't feel some kills were worthy of being painted. Others were put on canvas, but the artist was dissatisfied with his work and never displayed it. In other cases, he had already painted a specific type of bird but then found an intriguing individual variation, so he just had to blow it away.

He once wrote: "I call birds few when I shoot less than one hundred per day." ⌗

16
ONE-QUARTER OF LYNCHING VICTIMS WERE NOT BLACK

The word "lynch" has become synonymous with a white mob brutally killing a black person. The bulk of the time, lynchings did happen along those color lines. But not always. In a fourth of the known cases, a white, Asian, or Native person was the unfortunate victim.

The *Reader's Companion to American History* cites the universally referenced figures on mob hangings collected by the venerable Tuskegee Institute: "Between 1882 (when reliable statistics were first collected) and 1968 (when the classic forms of lynching had disappeared), 4,743 persons died of lynching, 3,446 of them black men and women." In other words, 27.3 percent were of other races.

The official website for the State of Texas says that in one the worst years (1885), lynch mobs in the state murdered 24 white people and 19 black people. In the year with the highest number of mob hangings (1892), 30 percent of the victims were white. In Kentucky, the overall tally was 31 percent white.

Naturally, it was almost always white mobs that killed white people, though there are a miniscule number of cases in which a black mob strung up a white person.

Also, we know of rare instances in which black mobs lynched black individuals. Eleven such incidents are known to have occurred in Georgia alone.

Most of the victims classified as "white" were US-born people of European extraction. However, this category also encompasses Mexicans (a minimum of 216 victims) and European immigrants. Some additional victims were targeted for being Jewish.

Adding further complexity are the victims of other races, including Native Americans and Chinese immigrants.

Although lynching was primarily white on black, the full picture — which has yet to be drawn but is hinted at here — shows that the contours of lynching aren't as simply rendered as we'd like to think. ⛝

17
FREUD FAILED TO HELP HIS PATIENTS

In his entire fabled career — which really is mostly a fable — Freud wrote up detailed case histories of only six patients, all of them heavily spun, revised, and embellished to make Herr Doktor look like a genius. In the intervening century or more, scholars have dug up documentation — such as letters and contemporaneous case notes — which demonstrate Freud's inability to meaningfully help his patients, falling light years short of the incredible cures he claimed.

Let's start by looking at the proto-case, "Anna O." Though she wasn't Freud's patient, students of the old man study the case because Anna was treated by his mentor, Josef Breur, and the case was later written up by Freud (though both of them attached their names to it). This is the founding case of psychotherapy — it supposedly validated hypnosis, "talking cures," repression, oedipal desire, and other pillars of this approach. The official story is that Anna was intensely neurotic and Breur completely rid her of her "hysteria" through hypnosis.

In actuality, one month after therapy ended, Breur had her committed to an insane asylum, a place she would stay three more times over the next five years. Breur considered her hopeless; in a letter to his fiancée, Freud related his mentor's thoughts on Anna: "Breur is constantly talking about her, says he wishes she were dead so that the poor woman could be free of her suffering. He says that she will never be well again, that she is completely shattered." (It turns out that Breur was wrong, because Anna did recover in the very late 1880s, around six or seven years after her therapy ended.) Not only did Breur and Freud keep these facts from the public, at Freud's insistence years later they fabricated the case history to make it fit with psychoanalysis, presenting this failure as a rousing success and attributing this nonexistent triumph to approaches and theories that weren't around at the time.

Now let's consider Freud's six detailed case histories, whose pseudonyms are household names to students of psychology.

The first case that Freud publicly presented as a cure — though it was far from his first case — was that of "Rat Man" (don't you love these psychiatric soubriquets?). Rat Man was obsessively afraid that something terrible would happen to his father and girlfriend; these morbid thoughts had started after he heard about a hideous form of torture involving rats. Freud's conclusion? Rat Man was repressing his desire to buttfuck his dad and future wife because — and this was an unconfirmed guess on the shrink's part — Ratty's dad had severely punished him for masturbating as a toddler.

In the case history, Sigmund claimed to have treated Rat Man for close to a year, but from his notes we know that the length was actually six months. Though Rat Man broke off the therapy, Freud boasted that he'd perfectly cured the fellow ("the complete restoration of the patient's personality"). But immediately after writing the case history, Freud told Jung in a letter that Rat Man was still messed up.

Five-year-old "Little Hans" suddenly became deathly afraid of horses. Though considered one of Freud's meager half-dozen case histories, Hans actually was treated by his father, a Freud disciple. Sigmund supervised the case from afar, seeing Hans only once. Young Hans was pretty sure that his horse phobia was due to trauma from seeing a horse fall down in the street, but his father and Freud would have none of this poppycock. It was obvious to them that big-dicked horses represented the lad's threatening father, whom Hans believed wanted to castrate him. Meanwhile, Hans also wanted to nail his mother and kill his kid sister. When pressed about his supposed desire toward mommy, Hans repeatedly said no way. But his dad kept hectoring him and, naturally, Little Hans eventually broke down and told him what he wanted to hear. "Success!" screamed the inquisitors. Actually, Hans *did* slowly lose his fear of horses during the treatment, but no one has to been able to produce a shred of evidence that the nutty therapy had anything to do with it, that it wasn't just Hans slowly recovering from his scary equestrian encounter.

Two of Freud's principal case histories are barely worth mentioning. Regarding Sigmund's treatment of an unnamed eighteen-year-old lesbian, MIT cognitive scientist Frank Sulloway —

author of *Freud: Biologist of the Mind* — writes that it "terminated after a short time and involved no therapeutic improvement or even real treatment." In the other case, Freud diagnosed a psychotic — whom he never met — strictly through the man's published memoir. Whether his conclusions were correct or not is impossible to say, but we do know that to arrive at them Freud ignored parts of the memoir that contradicted his diagnosis and purposely misrepresented the man's dad (in the case history, Freud lauded him as an "excellent father," while simultaneously admitting that he was a "despot" in a letter to a pupil).

"Dora" was a depressed and "hysterical" seventeen-year-old (not eighteen, as Freud claimed) who reluctantly came to Sigmund because of problems involving friends of the family, Mr. and Mrs. K. Dora was upset because 1) Mr. K. obviously wanted a piece of her and had even made passes at her when she was thirteen and sixteen, and 2) she rightly believed that her father and Mrs. K. were getting it on. The good doctor immediately sussed what was really happening: Not only was Dora in love with Mr. K., she also wanted to give her father a blowjob and hop into the sack with *Mrs*. K. Not surprisingly, Dora thought this was a load of crap and abruptly quit seeing Freud after eleven weeks. She was still a mess when she died.

The obsessive "Wolf Man" is Freud's best-known case, most often pointed to as a shining example of psychoanalysis. The entire thing hinges on a dream that the patient had as a child: He saw white wolves sitting on top of a tree in front of his bedroom window, then woke up terrified. From this, Freud deduced that Wolfie had seen his parents humping doggie-style when he was 18 months old.

It took Freud four years to treat this poor sap, who was eventually discharged as being fully cured. Decades later, an Austrian reporter tracked him down to find out how he'd been doing since his legendary headshrinking sessions. Wolf Man called Freud's dream interpretation "terribly farfetched"; the sex-peeping scenario, which he never remembered, was "improbable"; and the universal belief that he'd been cured was "false." Turns out that he continually saw a phalanx of therapists for the rest of his life. The psychoanalysis industry actively tried to hide the miserable failure of Freud's greatest so-called success by pressuring and financially inducing Wolf Man to stay in Vienna, instead of going to the US, as he wanted, because his status as a living piece of history would bring publicity and the truth would come out. He remained a bundle of neuroses and obsessions until his death.

As leading academic Freud debunker Frederick Crews writes: "Freud was unable to document a single unambiguously efficacious treatment." ⛝

18
THE BOARD GAME MONOPOLY
WAS SWIPED FROM QUAKERS

Monopoly, according to its manufacturer, has been played by over 500 million people. Translated into 26 languages, as well as Braille, it's sold 200 million copies as of 1999 (the latest figures the maker has announced). Over 5 billion of those green houses have been stamped, and each year countless dead trees are turned into 500 billion dollars of rainbow-hued money.

In other words, it's a popular game. The most successful board game ever.

The official story is that a toy tinkerer named Charles Darrow from Germantown, Pennsylvania, created this billion-dollar game out of whole cloth in 1934. However, the official story is what's made from whole cloth.

When economics professor Ralph Anspach cooked up a parody game called Anti-Monopoly — the goal is to bust trusts, not build them — Parker Brothers, not surprisingly, took him to court. While researching the game's history for the lawsuit, Anspach stumbled upon the hidden truth. Using dogged detective work, he assembled the suppressed history of Monopoly.

Greatly simplified, it goes like this. The roots stretch back to the Landlord's Game, a Monopolyesque game patented in 1904 by a cross-dressing Bohemian and game-inventor named Lizzie Magie. This game mutated into a folk-game called "monopoly." As charmingly quaint as it may seem, people used to spend hour after hour playing board games with each other; they would even handmake their own copies of a game's board, cards, and pieces. From 1910 to the early 1930s, this is what happened with monopoly, mainly in the Northeastern US.

While visiting her hometown of Indianapolis, Indiana, in 1929, a Quaker teacher named Ruth Hoskins was introduced to the game by a childhood friend. She made a copy, which she took back to Atlantic City, New Jersey. Her friends and colleagues, themselves Quakers, soon decided to redo the game using places from their neck of the woods — Pacific Avenue, Park Place, the Boardwalk, etc. They also added the little hotels in addition to houses. In a crucial rule change, they removed the property auctions and gave each piece of pretend real estate a fixed value, making the game so simple that even little kids could play.

Eventually, a Quaker couple invited another couple to play the game. That's how Charles Darrow was introduced to monopoly. He showed great interest, pressing his hosts to explain all the fine points of the game. When he asked them to type up the rules and make a board for him, they thought he was a demanding bastard, but they complied. Next thing you know, Darrow is selling it as a game he "created." He had lifted the Quakers' Atlantic City version wholesale, making only some superficial changes to the game board (such as putting a colored stripe across the top of the squares instead of the original colored triangles in the bottom left corner).

He then sold it to Parker Brothers, still pretending to have invented it. The company soon discovered the ruse but went along with it, omitting and suppressing evidence of the game's true origins when they patented it under Darrow's name.

In its ruling against Parker Brothers' effort to torpedo Anti-Monopoly, the Ninth Circuit Court of

Appeals officially agreed with the facts that Anspach unearthed, declaring that the "reference to Darrow as the inventor or creator of the game is clearly erroneous." The Supreme Court upheld the decision.

Even today, Hasbro — which assimilated Parker Brothers — won't acknowledge the origins of their cash cow. They have, however, craftily modified their so-called history of Monopoly. The game's website now coyly refers to the "legend" of the game's birth, which commences when Darrow "showed" the game to the suits at Parker Brothers. They don't say that he created it, although that's the impression you'd get if you didn't know the real story. ▯

19
GANDHI REFUSED TO LET HIS DYING WIFE TAKE PENICILLIN YET TOOK QUININE TO SAVE HIMSELF

Gandhi is often ranked, directly or subtly, alongside Jesus Christ and Martin Luther King, Jr. as one of the greatest peacemakers — indeed, one of the greatest human beings — of all time. The mythology that surrounds him — which he built, leaving his followers, admirers, and hagiographers to reinforce and embellish — has almost completely smothered the many unflattering facts about him.

In such a compact book, space doesn't permit a full exploration of Gandhi's numerous, consequential skeletons — his racism toward blacks and whites, his betrayal of the Untouchables, his acquiescence toward the Nazis. Instead, let's focus on something more personal and, in some ways, more upsetting.

In August 1942, Gandhi and his wife, Kasturba, among others, were imprisoned by the British in Aga Khan Palace near Poona. Kasturba had poor circulation, and she'd weathered several heart attacks. While detained in the palace, she developed bronchial pneumonia. One of her four sons, Devadas, wanted her to take penicillin. Gandhi refused. He was okay with her receiving traditional remedies, such as water from the Ganges, but he refused her any medicines, including this newfangled antibiotic, saying that the Almighty would have to heal her.

The Life and Death of Mahatma Gandhi quotes him on February 19, 1944: "If God wills it, He will pull her through." *Gandhi: A Life* adds this wisdom from the Mahatma: "You cannot cure your mother now, no matter what wonder drugs you may muster. She is in God's hands now." Three days later, Devadas was still pushing for the penicillin, but Gandhi shot back: "Why don't you trust God?" Kasturba died that day.

The next night, Gandhi cried out: "But how God tested *my* faith!" He told one of Kasturba's doctors that the antibiotic wouldn't have saved her and that allowing her to have it "would have meant the bankruptcy of *my* faith." (Emphasis mine.)

But Gandhi's faith wasn't much of an obstacle a short time later when it was his ass on the line. A mere six weeks after Kasturba died, Gandhi was flattened by malaria. He stuck to an all-liquid diet as his doctors tried to convince him to take quinine. But Gandhi completely refused and died of the disease, right? No, actually, after three weeks of deterioration, he took the diabolical drug and quickly recovered. That stuff about trusting God's will and testing faith only applied when his wife's life hung in the balance. When he needed a drug to stave off the Grim Reaper, down the hatch it went. ☐

20
SEVERAL THOUSAND AMERICANS WERE HELD IN NAZI CONCENTRATION CAMPS

During the Nazi era, Europeans weren't the only ones who ended up in concentration and slave-labor camps. Americans were also sent there. What's more, the US government knew but decided to take no action.

This untidy bit of history had been hidden for decades. Even with the still-growing mountain of literature on the Holocaust, the fate of Americans has been almost entirely ignored, garnering only a few passing mentions. After stumbling across these shards of an ignored truth, Mitchell G. Bard, PhD, did some serious archival research and conducted fresh interviews, resulting in *Forgotten Victims*, the only book to address the subject.

Bard estimates that "probably a few thousand" US citizens, mainly Jews, spent time in Hitler's camps. Hundreds died there. "American Jews," he explains, "were subject to the same anti-Semitic regulations and dangers as any other Jews who came under control of the Nazis."

Some of the victims were American civilians living in Europe at the wrong time. The State Department sent a total of nine ships during 1939 and 1940 to ferry back Americans living on the Continent. As documents from the time period make clear, State officials believed that Americans who didn't get on those boats deserved whatever happened to them. Around 2,000 of them landed in concentration camps, with at least 200 Jewish Americans ending up in a single one. Small numbers were reported in Dachau and Auschwitz, and some Americans, perhaps dozens, were trapped in the infamous Warsaw ghetto.

Bard further proves that US officials knew *while events were happening* that American citizens were in Nazi camps, prisons, and ghettos, yet they purposely refused to take action. The reasons for this policy of deliberate indifference were varied: These citizens might act as Axis spies. If we act to get American Jews out of harm's way, then *all* Jews will want the same help. Pure pettiness was also to blame: The government seemed miffed that these Americans had chosen to live abroad. In other words, they made their bed; let them die in it.

Captured Allied soldiers were principally kept at POW camps, but several hundred American prisoners of war, some Jewish, were shipped to concentration camps, including Buchenwald, Mauthausen, and the slave labor camp at Berga. Some were summarily executed or worked to death. The US government pled ignorance, but the paper trail shows that at the very least they knew what was happening in Berga. After the war, when the POWs were debriefed, some even giving depositions, the official response was reprehensible. "The government denied many of these atrocities took place," Bard notes, "resisted compensating them for their injuries and failed to bring the perpetrators to justice."

21
THE US HAS ALMOST NUKED CANADA, BRITAIN, SPAIN, GREENLAND, AND TEXAS

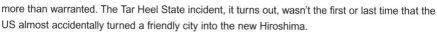

While giving lots of interviews for the release of the first volume of *50 Things*, by far the most popular topic was the accidental nuclear bombing of North Carolina in 1961. It struck such a nerve that a follow-up is more than warranted. The Tar Heel State incident, it turns out, wasn't the first or last time that the US almost accidentally turned a friendly city into the new Hiroshima.

The first such mishap occurred over Canada. On February 13, 1950, a B-36 from Alaska iced up while flying over Vancouver. Before bailing out, the crew veered over the Pacific and dropped their nuclear bomb right off the coast. The conventional explosives detonated, but luckily they didn't trigger a nuclear reaction.

The Royal Air Force Station Lakenheath, around 80 miles from London, was the site of a close call on July 26, 1956. A number of US planes were housed at the base for strategic reasons. One of them, a B-47, crashed and burned while attempting to land. It skidded into a storage building housing three atomic bombs, its blazing fuel setting everything on fire. Each bomb was loaded with four tons of TNT, but the fire was put out before the Mark VI's became dirty bombs.

A telex from the General in charge, declassified decades later, said: "Preliminary exam by bomb disposal officer says a miracle that one Mark Six with exposed detonators didn't go off." When the incident finally came to light, a retired Air Force Major General told a reporter: "It is possible that a part of Eastern England would have become a desert."

A B-47 caught fire and crashed during takeoff in Texas on November 4, 1958. Again, the explosives on the nuke went kaboom, but there was no mushroom cloud explosion.

Spain was the site of the worst such disaster. While refueling over the coastal village of Palomares on January 17, 1966, two planes collided and blew up. The B-52 was carrying four nuclear weapons. One landed safely near the village; another was lost at sea. Three months later, it was fished out of 2,850 feet of water. "The search took about eighty days and employed 3,000 Navy personnel and 33 Navy vessels," according to the Center for Defense Information, "not including ships, planes, and people used to move equipment to the site." The other two A-bombs landed in fields, their explosives went off, and 558 acres were contaminated with plutonium. As part of its contrition, the US military packed 1,400 tons of radioactive dirt into steel drums, then shipped the glowing mess back to the States for disposal. To this day, the Department of Energy still monitors the health of the people and the land.

Two years later (January 21, 1968), a B-52 headed toward Thule US Air Force Base in Greenland crashed seven miles away. Three of the four nukes on board exploded, spritzing plutonium over a large area. In a replay of the Palomares aftermath, 237,000 cubic feet of snow, ice, and debris were packed into drums and freighted to the US for disposal. The evidence conflicts over whether the fourth bomb, which went into the ocean, was recovered or is still underwater.

And this isn't even close to the whole list. There have been many other close calls — crashes of nuke-bearing planes in Kentucky, New Mexico, and Morocco; the jettisoning of two A-bombs off the Delaware coast (never recovered) and one near Tybee Island, Georgia (also never recovered). Then there are the nuclear oopsie-daisies committed by Britain and the Soviet Union. It seems likely that every nuclear power — including France and Israel — must've had similar nail-biting moments, though they've been kept hush-hush. ⌗

22
DURING THE COLD WAR, THE CODE TO UNLOCK NUCLEAR MISSILES WAS "00000000"

Missiles being moved around may have presented a few Maalox moments, but when they were in the silos, they were safe and secure, right? You're not gonna launch these babies without bunches of people going through bunches of complicated steps, especially once Defense Secretary Robert McNamara put technical locks on the Minutemen nukes around 1961. Except that the Strategic Air Command thought the eight-digit combinations necessary to launch intercontinental ballistic missiles were for candy-asses, the kind of fraidy-cats who engage the safety on their personal firearms. So the combination for all the missiles was kept at "00000000."

This was revealed by Bruce G. Blair, PhD, who was a Minuteman launch officer during this period. Now the head of the Center for Defense Information, he says: "Our launch checklist in fact instructed us, the firing crew, to double-check the locking panel in our underground launch bunker to ensure that no digits other than zero had been inadvertently dialed into the panel."

When Blair told McNamara about this in 2004, the old warmonger went ballistic. "I am shocked, absolutely shocked and outraged," he blustered. "Who the hell authorized that?"

The locks were finally given legitimate combinations in 1977. ☐

23
THE GOVERNMENT PRACTICALLY GIVES AWAY VALUABLE LAND TO CORPORATE INTERESTS

It stands to reason that land loaded with gold, silver, platinum, palladium, and other prized minerals would command huge prices. But, as with so many other things, reason has nothing to do with it. The government sells the rights to mine public land for amounts that a schoolkid could buy with allowance money.

It happens under the 1872 Mining Law, which set the prices for mineral rights. Unfortunately, nobody has updated the amounts in the intervening 130+ years, which means that we're stuck with a ridiculous situation.

Just how ridiculous? The Environmental Working Group spent a year gathering data and crunching numbers on the mineral rights to public land in the eleven westernmost states of the continental US, plus Montana.

Depending on how many acres are at issue, you can snatch the mineral rights to public land for

84 cents to $6.75 per acre, with a yearly renewal fee of 52 cents to $5 an acre.

Since 1992, Congress has tacked on an additional $100 annual renewal fee per tract of land (not per acre), but even this token effort is a stop-gap measure. They have yet to make it permanent.

Just to make things even more absurd, it's been possible to outright *buy* the public land, not just the right to mine it, for a little more: $4.06 to $17.10 per acre, depending on total number of acres and the type of mining you want to do. Each year since 1994, Congress has passed an annual moratorium on the ability to purchase land this way, but it refuses to permanently ban the practice.

When the Working Group published its report in 2004, the mining rights for almost 5,570,000 acres of public land had been claimed this way. On top of that, an additional 3,718,000 acres had been flat-out purchased through this form of legalized theft. All told, these lands are controlled by over 26,000 individuals, 2,270 US companies, and 94 foreign companies. (These non-US corporations own over one-fifth of the claimed lands.) As in most things economic, concentration rears its head: "Ten companies and individuals control 21 percent of claimed lands on US public lands," says the EWG.

The owners of the mineral rights and/or the land itself have to plunk down only the nominal fees listed above; they pay the US nothing based on the value of the minerals they mine (in other words, no "royalties" like those rendered by coal, gas, and oil companies). Theoretically, the government could at least see some money based on taxes of the resulting corporate profits, but since the majority of corporations don't pay income tax, this revenue stream is nothing more than a trickle.

As the icing on this demented cake, the government (read: taxpayers) ends up footing the bill for dealing with the pollution and devastation caused by the private mining of these so-called public lands. The mining of metal requires a tiny 0.36 percent of all "industrial facilities," yet it accounts for 46 percent of all industrial pollution.

The Working Group points out some ludicrous real-life examples of the 1872 Mining Law in action:

Land in Crested Butte, Colorado — a ski resort town — goes for a million dollars per acre. The government sold land nearby for $5.64 an acre. The mining company that bought the primo real estate for pocket money estimated that it would net $158 million over the next eleven years.

The Canadian corporation Barrick Gold paid a measly $10,000 for 1,800 acres of Nevada containing an estimated 17.5 million ounces of gold. Bruce Babbit, then Secretary of the Interior, resisted the sale until forced by a court order to proceed. He summed up: "What I'm wondering is why I'm giving $10 billion of the…assets owned by American citizens to a company that's not even an American company?"

A joint mining venture of Chevron and Stillwater Mining Company scored an even bigger take. For their $10,000, they outright bought 1,800 acres of national forest in Montana. As the Working Group points out, they "gained platinum and palladium reserves worth more than $35 billion, a return of $3.5 million for every one dollar received by the federal government."

In some cases, individuals have grabbed public land for a pittance, then sold it for a fortune. One case involves Yucca Mountain, which will soon be home to the nuclear waste of the entire country. When the location of this toxic super-storage facility was announced, some person hot-footed it to the appropriate government office and laid claim to some of the land. Instead of holding onto it to block the plans for an atomic waste dump, he forced the government to pay $250,000 to get back its land.

As noted above, Congress passes temporary measures to make the law's application less ridiculous, but they're too beholden to powerful corporate interests to do anything forceful and lasting. ♡

24
MOST CORPORATIONS PAY NO FEDERAL INCOME TAX

The fact that most corporations in the US don't pay federal income tax is one of those things that all of us have heard, but we're not sure just how true it is. It's completely true, and now we have the exact figures from the pro-business *Wall Street Journal* and the famously neutral General Accounting Office (an investigative arm of Congress now known as the Government Accountability Office).

The GAO examined millions of tax returns from 1996 through 2000, the economic boom years. They found that 61 percent of

US-based corporations paid no income tax. For foreign-controlled corporations that operate in the US, 71 percent didn't pay.

When they looked strictly at "large" corporations — "those with assets of at least $250 million or gross receipts of at least $50 million in constant 2000 dollars" — the percentages are switched, with 71 percent of large US corporations and 61 percent of large foreign-controlled businesses not contributing to the country's coffers.

To make it even more sickening, most of the corporations that actually do owe taxes pay a rate less than 5 percent, even though the base rate for corporate entities is 35 percent. (Only 0.6 percent of US corporations and 0.1 percent of non-US corporations paid 30 percent or more, the suckers.)

So when you add the corporations that pay no taxes with those that pay tiny taxes, 94 percent of US-controlled companies and 89 percent of foreign-controlled companies paid zero to 4 percent in taxes.

To make sure these numbers weren't due to small businesses that broke even or went belly-up, the bean counters looked at the stats for large corporations only. In this category, 82 percent of US-controlled companies and 76 percent of foreign-controlled companies paid less than 5 percent in taxes.

This failure to pony up their fair share is killing the government's bottom line. The *WSJ* reports:

Corporate tax receipts have shrunk markedly as a share of overall federal revenue in recent years, and were particularly depressed when the economy soured. By 2003, they had fallen to just 7.4% of overall federal receipts, the lowest rate since 1983, and the second-lowest rate since 1934, federal budget officials say. ⌑

25
THE MILITARY USED TO PUT SLANDEROUS SECRET CODES ON DISCHARGE PAPERS

When you're discharged from the US military, your personnel file contains a form DD-214, "Report of Separation." It summarizes your service and shows what type of discharge you received. For decades, it secretly revealed much more than that.

Starting in 1947, the US military put a Separation Program Number (SPN) — typically three or four digits, letters, or a combination — on this final piece of paperwork. Unbeknownst to the veterans, this cryptic code revealed *exactly* why they had left the armed forces.

Some of the 500+ codes, especially those developed at the outset, aren't damaging or problematic. They simply indicate run-of-the-mill reasons for leaving the service. For example, "201" means that an enlisted person's term of service ended; "RE-3S" shows that the vet was a family's only surviving son; and "627" indicates that the vet hit the upper age limit and was let go. Most codes, though, are very invasive of privacy. Here are the meanings of some SPN codes:

- admission of homosexuality or bisexuality • alcoholism • anti-social • AWOL, desertion
- bedwetter • criminalism • discreditable incidents - civilian or military • drug use
- failure of selection for promotion • financial irresponsibility • indebtedness
- interest of national security • obesity • pregnancy • resignation of enlisted personnel on unspecified enlistment in lieu of separation for disloyalty or subversion • schizoid personality
- security reason • separation for concealment of serious arrest record
- sexual deviate • sexual perversion • shirking • unfitness: homosexual acts
- unsanitary habits • withdrawal of ecclesiastical endorsement

Who decided what code to assign, which scarlet letter would follow a vet for the rest of his or her life? In most cases, it was the service member's commanding officer, who had a free hand in the matter. The SPNs weren't given only to people who got dishonorable or other-than-honorable discharges — they were affixed to everyone's record, even those who received honorable or general discharges.

When the existence and purpose of SPNs were officially admitted in 1973, it was further revealed that many employers were well aware of what each code meant. Job applicants who were vets had to make their DD-214's available to potential employers, who would then ask the Pentagon or look up the codes in lists that had been published in obscure, unclassified military documents.

SPNs were vanquished in 1974, due to pressure from Democratic Congressmen. However, vets discharged during the SPN period will still have this marker on their DD-214 unless they specifically request that the military reissue their separation report without the ratfink code. ⌑

26
ONE IN THREE AMERICAN HOMELESS MEN IS A MILITARY VETERAN

The US Department of Veterans Affairs reveals: "On any given day, as many as 250,000 veterans (male and female) are living on the streets or in shelters, and perhaps twice as many experience homelessness at some point during the course of a year." That's an awful lot, and the situation is even bleaker when you look at the percentages.

Veterans comprise 6 percent of the overall population, but they're 23 percent of the homeless. Of all homeless men, one-third are vets.

Forty-six percent of homeless vets are 45 or older, compared to 20 percent of the civilian homeless.

The VA says that "the number of homeless male and female Vietnam era veterans is greater than the number of service persons who died during that war."

Though almost half of homeless vets (47 percent) served during 'Nam, they've also served in WWII and every war since, not to mention during peacetime. The National Coalition for Homeless Veterans cites federal figures: "More than 67% served our country for at least three years and 33% were stationed in a war zone."

Peter Dougherty, Director of Homeless Veterans Programs at the VA, candidly told the *Los*

Angeles Times: "Traditionally, what happens to you after you leave has not been a concern of [the] service."

To give some credit, the VA and Defense Department are doing a little to change that, but they still reach only 20 to 25 percent of homeless vets. Many nonprofits are trying to fill the gap, from the above-mentioned National Coalition for Homeless Veterans to local efforts, such as the New England Shelter for Homeless Veterans in Boston. ⌕

27
THE US IMPRISONS MORE OF ITS POPULATION THAN ANY OTHER COUNTRY

The United States is home to almost 5 percent of the world's population, yet it holds 22 percent of the world's prisoners.

The latest official statistics show that as of the middle of 2003, federal, state, and local facilities in America were holding 2,078,570 people.

If we add those on parole or probation, the figure jumps to 6.9 million.

For the last 30 years, the number of prisoners has increased annually. The incarcerated population in mid-2003 is a 2.9 percent rise over the prior year. Currently, one of every 75 men is in the clink.

Not only are the absolute numbers sky-high and ever-increasing, but the rate of imprisonment keeps climbing into higher nosebleed territory, too. In mid-2003, the US imprisoned 709 people out of every 100,000. A year and a half earlier, that figure was 686.

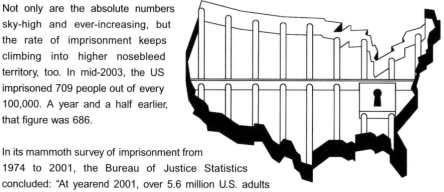

In its mammoth survey of imprisonment from 1974 to 2001, the Bureau of Justice Statistics concluded: "At yearend 2001, over 5.6 million U.S. adults had ever served time in State or Federal prison. If incarceration rates remain unchanged, 6.6% of U.S. residents born in 2001 will go to prison at some time during their lifetime."

These numbers are not only the highest among industrialized nations, they're the highest in the world. The British government's definitive study "World Prison Population List" (fourth edition, 2003) gives the following top five prison nations as of the start of 2002:

US: 686 inmates per 100,000 people
Cayman Islands: 664 • Russia: 638 • Belarus: 554 • Kazakhstan: 522

In Cuba, the rate is approximately 297. Meanwhile, in lovely Iran, the incarceration rate is 229. The US's northern neighbor has a rate of 102, while South of the border, it's 156. England and

Wales combined have a rate of 139. The figures are even lower in Scotland (126) and Northern Ireland (62). The rates for other nations that are interesting for comparison purposes:

Ukraine: 406 • South Africa: 404 • Israel: 153 • Spain: 126 • Australia: 116 • China: 111
Saudi Arabia: 110 • Germany: 96 • Italy: 95 • Uganda: 91 • France: 85 • Vietnam: 71
Japan: 48 • Nigeria: 34 • India: 28

So why does the US keep record numbers of its people in cages? The field of criminal justice is wrestling with that question, and the answers are complicated, but among the biggest factors are an ever-increasing number of laws, mandatory sentencing, and the so-called War on Drugs (drug offenders make up around half the federal prison population). ⌼

28
THE GOVERNMENT CAN TAKE YOUR PROPERTY WITHOUT EVEN CHARGING YOU WITH A CRIME

If law enforcement officials even suspect that you're involved in a crime, usually a drug-related one, they can seize your property and keep it. You don't have to be convicted of the crime. In fact, you don't even have to be *charged* with one.

This despotic power, known as asset forfeiture, is widely known (and decried) in many alternative circles, but it has yet to seep into the mainstream consciousness. That's too bad, because it's not a fringe issue but something that has the potential to affect any of us, no matter how law-abiding.

The most likely way an innocent person will get snared in this nightmare is by living with someone — a family member, significant other, or roommate — who's involved with drugs. This is what happened in Albuquerque, New Mexico, in March 2004. Police raided a home occupied by two men, one allegedly involved in the drug trade, the other not. The police busted open a safe in the innocent guy's room, took the $10,000 cash he had received because of a car accident, and kept it. He's suing to get it back.

A month earlier, the *St. Petersburg Times* reported the case of a woman whose acquaintance had stashed a pound of pot in her car without her knowledge. The cops told her that if she signed over her ride, they wouldn't prosecute her. Scared to death, she agreed. When the media started questioning the police about this, they gave back the car. The woman's lawyer said: "This is like a mob shakedown."

Sometimes it's pretty obvious that the property really was knowingly used in commission of crimes. The Border Patrol seizes hundreds upon hundreds of vehicles apparently being used to smuggle people from Mexico into the US. But even in these cases, seizure is a blatantly unconstitutional violation of due process rights. The officers become judge, jury, and executioner.

Federal, state, and local law enforcement agencies all have their own forfeiture programs. At the top level, the Justice Department and the Treasury Department handle this legalized theft. In a report to Congress, Justice tallied the amount of money, real estate, vehicles, art, and other possessions that were "forfeited" in fiscal year 2003: $466,968,207 worth. The Treasury sets its total for the same year at $687,761,000. Well over a billion dollars in one year, and that's just at the federal level.

The Justice Department's website explains the three types of forfeiture. Criminal forfeiture involves a jury and a judge; it's used in the criminal prosecution of individuals and is the hardest form to abuse. In civil judicial forfeiture, a court is also involved but, as Justice explains, "no criminal charge against the owner is necessary." Finally, we have administrative forfeiture, the most egregious variety, in which the feds just snatch people's property. In the words of the Justice Department, it "permits the federal seizing agency to forfeit the property *without judicial involvement.*" It's then up to you to prove that your possessions were wrongly taken.

The practice has its roots in the admiralty laws of England, then America, which hold that inanimate objects can be considered guilty of crimes. The US Supreme Court has upheld this silliness since 1796, and numerous laws from the 1970s and 1980s — such as the RICO conspiracy statutes — only strengthened the practice. The website of the US Marshals Service notes the existence of "more than 200 federal laws that have forfeiture provisions." The Civil Asset Forfeiture Reform Act of 2000 has helped curb the most wanton abuses, though the practice continues. ⌁

29
THE EPA LIED ABOUT NEW YORK'S AIR QUALITY AFTER 9/11

When the Twin Towers of the World Trade Center collapsed on 9/11, humongous plumes of concrete dust, asbestos, lead, and other material hovered over Manhattan. Fires at the site burned for over two months, releasing even more junk, like dioxins, PCBs, and volatile organic compounds.

Yet the Environmental Protection Agency painted a rosy picture of air quality. On September 13, 2001, an EPA press release cheerily said that the results of their testing were "very reassuring" and "uniformly acceptable." Administrator Christine Todd Whitman was quoted: "EPA is greatly relieved to have learned that there appears to be no significant levels of asbestos dust in the air in New York City."

The next day, the EPA's missive soothed frazzled nerves: "EPA continues to believe that there is no significant health risk to the general public in the coming days." On the 18th of that month, Whitman declared: "I am glad to reassure the people of New York and Washington, D.C. that their air is safe to breathe..."

It was all a lie.

The first revelation came in the form of a report from the EPA's Inspector General. The internal watchdog said that at the time the EPA made these pronouncements, it simply didn't have enough data to know whether or not the air was kosher. Of the fourteen toxic substances believed to present the most danger, the EPA didn't have results for ten of them until a week or more after the attacks (that is, after the statement that the "air is safe"). Of the ones it did have, the EPA used imprecise testing methods and incorrect benchmarks.

The report also revealed that the White House had pressured the agency into making its calming claims and had ordered the removal of some precautionary statements, despite the health risks to the public. Additionally, the EPA press releases had to be cleared by the National Security Council before being disseminated.

A leaked memo by Cate Jenkins, PhD, a scientist in the EPA's Office of Solid Waste, exposes additional layers of deceit. She shows that on 9/11 and afterward, tests by the EPA, Con Edison, and others did indeed show that asbestos levels were leaps and bounds above 0.1 percent (the level which EPA considers problematic, requiring action). A level of 4.49 percent was found two blocks from Ground Zero the day after the attacks. On 9/16 and 9/17, at a location sixteen blocks away, tests found a level of 3 percent. One block north, almost two weeks after the attacks, tests measured a whopping 5 percent. All the talk of "reassuring," "acceptable," and "safe" levels was hogwash, and the agency knew it.

Jenkins also reveals: "EPA dismissed levels of toxins such as dioxins as being 'very low' or 'below the detection limit' despite the fact that levels of dioxin measured in the air many blocks away from Ground Zero were the highest ever detected in outdoor air."

The EPA told NY residents that not only didn't they need professional cleaning of their homes and offices, they could clean up the dust, laden with asbestos and other toxins, *on their own* with mops and wet rags. People didn't even need to wear dust masks while doing this. Yet, at the exact same time the EPA was broadcasting these suicidal instructions, the agency had its Manhattan office building professionally cleansed of asbestos. (Not only that, the EPA employed a sensitive, high-tech method to test for asbestos in its building, while it used only an older, less sensitive method for the rest of Manhattan. To add another insult to the mix, the EPA gave its employees gasmasks to use inside its building, while assuring everyone else that they didn't even need the cheap painters masks you can buy at hardware stores.)

Further actions on the part of the EPA are just as inexplicably callous. In 1998, when one floor of a federal building in Manhattan was contaminated with asbestos from insulation, the EPA tested 4,000 to 5,000 samples *on that floor alone*. How many samples did it test in all of Manhattan after 9/11? Around 250.

And some people still crinkle their brows, unable to comprehend why so many of us don't trust the government.... ♡

30
CONDOLEEZZA RICE COMMITTED PERJURY BEFORE THE 9/11 COMMISSION

During her April 8, 2004, appearance before the 9/11 Commission, National Security Adviser Condoleezza Rice discussed the infamous Presidential Daily Brief of August 6, 2001. At the time, the document was still classified. We did, however, know the title: "Bin Ladin Determined to Strike In US."

Rice was asked by commission member Richard Ben-Veniste: "Isn't it a fact, Dr. Rice, that the August 6 PDB warned against possible attacks in this country?"

Keeping in mind that Rice was under oath, read her reply:

"You said, did it not warn of attacks. It did not warn of attacks inside the United States. It was historical information based on old reporting. There was no new

threat information. And it did not, in fact, warn of any coming attacks inside the United States."

In the continuing testy exchange, she reiterated: "Commissioner, this was not a warning. This was a historic memo…"

Then she gets specific about how nonspecific the memo was: "But I can also tell you that there was nothing in this memo that suggested that an attack was coming on New York or Washington, D.C."

So here we have the President's top adviser on security swearing before God and country that the memo "Bin Ladin Determined to Strike In US" did not discuss Bin Laden's plans to strike in the US.

It seemed absolutely ridiculous, but we had to take her word for it. Not for long, though. Two days later — under intense pressure — the White House miraculously released the document, 99 percent uncensored. Some of the short memo did discuss the past (this was the "historical information" part) but only as a way of emphasizing Bin Laden's continuing willingness to attack America. The briefing says that this illustrates his patience, his tactic of planning strikes for years. His earlier plots were just the first part of his plans to attack inside the US itself, the memo warns. In bold italics, it blares: "Al-Qa'ida members — including some who are US citizens — have resided in or traveled to the US for years, and the group apparently maintains a support structure that could aid attacks."

This all builds up to the crescendo of the last two paragraphs, which explicitly warn that plots are underway:

... FBI information since that time indicates patterns of suspicious activity in this country consistent with preparations for hijacking or other types of attacks, including recent surveillance of federal buildings in New York.

The FBI is conducting approximately 70 full field investigations throughout the US that it considers Bin Ladin-related. CIA and the FBI are investigating a call to our Embassy in the UAE [United Arab Emirates] in May saying that a group of Bin Ladin supporters was in the US planning attacks with explosives.

This is the "historical" memo that contained "no new threat information." The briefing that "did not warn of attacks inside the United States," certainly not anything about an attack on New York.

When mere mortals lie under oath, it's called perjury. When National Security Advisers lie under oath to Congressionally-mandated commissions, it's called...nothing, really. Because no one mentions it.

It's worth noting that Bush also lied about the warning memo, claiming that the "PDB said nothing about an attack on America." ⌖

31
AL QAEDA ATTACKS HAVE INCREASED SUBSTANTIALLY SINCE 9/11

Despite the very costly "War on Terror" — which, we are repeatedly assured, is making the world safer than ever before — attacks by al Qaeda have skyrocketed. This supposedly "decimated" network of terrorists has been busier, and more deadly, than ever *after* the attacks of September 11, 2001.

The famously neutral, thorough Congressional Research Service — whose reports are almost never made available to the general public — looked at the number of al Qaeda attacks perpetrated in the two and a half years after 9/11, balanced against the number of attacks during that amount of time before 9/11.

While some experts believe that there's no such thing as "al Qaeda," that the term was created by the CIA to refer to groups, cells, and individuals that have little, if anything, to do with each other, the CRS looked at incidents that the government credits to al Qaeda. Thus, under the establishment's own rules of the game, al Qaeda's attacks went from *one* in the 30 months before 9/11, to *ten* during the 30 months after 9/11.

The discrepancy is even worse when you look at the number of fatalities. Before 9/11: 17 deaths. After 9/11: 510 deaths.

When comparing injuries, the difference becomes 64-fold. In the 30 months before 9/11, al Qaeda injured 39 people. In the 30 months after, it injured 2,526.

The differences can be considered even more lopsided because the one pre-9/11 attack was the bombing of the *USS Cole* in Yemen. The report explains that "some experts do not include this attack as a 'terrorist incident,' because it was directed against a military, not civilian, target, although the Cole was not engaged in combat during that period." One of the post-9/11 attacks was against military personnel in Kuwait. So if we take out the two military attacks, the scorecard is zero to nine.

Even if we lengthen the time period to look at *all* al Qaeda attacks prior to 9/11, the news is still bad. Al Qaeda's first attack took place in December 1992. During the almost nine years until 9/11, there were four attacks, two of which were against military targets: the *Cole* and US servicemen in Somalia.

So, the final tally:

Two attacks against civilian targets and two against military targets in the nine years prior to 9/11.

Nine attacks against civilian targets and one against a military target in the two and a half years after 9/11. ⌑

32
THE PATRIOT ACT IS USED IN CASES THAT HAVE NOTHING TO DO WITH TERRORISM

We were assured that the USA Patriot Act would be wielded only to nab terrorists. After all, in the law's full, convoluted name — Uniting and Strengthening America by Providing Appropriate Tools Required to Intercept and Obstruct Terrorism Act — the *only* crime mentioned is terrorism. According to US Representative Ron Paul (R-TX), Congress, shaken by 9/11, didn't even read the gargantuan bill before passing it. They apparently bought the line that it was necessary to prevent more attacks and voted for it sight unseen.

Attorney General John Ashcroft, in defending the act — which he frequently has to do — only mentions its role in terrorism. In his speeches about it, he says the following (or something almost exactly like it):

"The Patriot Act does three things: First, it closes the gaping holes in our ability to investigate *terrorists*. Second, the Patriot Act updates our *anti-terrorism* laws to meet the challenges of new technology, and new threats. Third, the Patriot Act has allowed us to build an extensive team that shares information and fights *terrorism* together."

In another speech, he invoked 9/11: "Armed with the tools provided by the Patriot Act, the men and women of justice and law enforcement have dedicated themselves to the unfinished work of those who resisted, those who assisted, and those who sacrificed on September 11th."

He told Congress: "Our ability to prevent another catastrophic attack on American soil would be more difficult, if not impossible, without the Patriot Act. It has been the key weapon used across America in successful counter-terrorist operations to protect innocent Americans from the deadly plans of terrorists."

When he signed the legislation into law, President Bush said: "These terrorists must be pursued, they must be defeated, and they must be brought to justice. And that is the purpose of this legislation."

Get it? It's all about terrorism. In all of their speeches and public comments, Ashcroft and Bush never even faintly whispered about any other use of the Patriot Act. But those other uses have been legion.

Around two years after 9/11, unnamed Justice Department officials admitted that the act has been applied in "hundreds" of cases that had nothing to do with terrorism.

The Patriot Act was used to investigate allegations that an owner of two Las Vegas titty clubs was bribing local officials. The feds invoked section 314 of the act to get financial records of the parties under suspicion. That particular part of the act applies to people suspected "of engaging in terrorist acts or money laundering activities." Notice the weasel-word "or." They can be engaged in terrorism *or* they can be laundering money for any purpose under the Sun.

Section 319 of the law was used to get money from a lawyer indicted on charges of bilking his clients. He skipped the country and allegedly put a wad of cash in Belizean banks. When Belize refused to turn over the dough, the feds invoked the Patriot Act to seize $1.7 million from the banks' accounts in the US.

The owner of a fan website devoted to the sci-fi show *Stargate SG-1* posted streaming video of episodes for download. MGM and the Motion Picture Association of America called in the FBI for this alleged copyright violation, and they whipped out the Patriot Act to get the webmaster's financial records from his ISP.

From January through October 2003, a computer science grad student in Madison, Wisconsin, disrupted emergency radio frequencies over a several block radius. One of his feats was to broadcast X-rated recordings over police radios. The student was considered intellectually gifted but socially retarded, and even the US Assistant Attorney who prosecuted the case said that the "immaturity of the defendant" was the motivator, not terrorism. Nonetheless, prosecuted under section 814 of the Patriot Act, which covers "cyberterrorism," the radio hacker got eight years in the slammer.

A Mexican citizen who pled guilty to attempting to smuggle over $824,000 from Alabama to his home country was nailed under a Patriot Act provision covering the reporting of currency.

The expanded surveillance capabilities of the act were also used to break up two rings of child pornographers/molesters, to track down a man who had abducted and sexually assaulted his estranged wife, and to break up an ecstasy-smuggling operation.

Additionally, the Justice Department has exploited the Patriot Act to:

- bust scammers who steal credit card info over the Net;
- find a woman who had been kidnapped;
- pinch a hacker who stole a company's trade secrets.

Further, the *New York Times* reported: "Authorities also have used their expanded authority to track private Internet communications in order to investigate a major drug distributor, a four-time killer, an identity thief and a fugitive who fled on the eve of trial by using a fake passport."

Just give us these powers, the authorities said, and we'll only use them to nail evil-doing terrorists, to avenge those killed on 9/11, to keep Ma and Pa Kettle safe from the brown hordes of al Qaeda. But now these expanded powers are being against hackers, bribers, copyright violators, con artists, kidnappers, killers, child pornographers, cash smugglers, ecstasy makers, and radio jammers. And that's just what's we know about.

Not that the end result of busting some of these characters is a bad thing in and of itself. But if these new powers of law enforcement are so wonderful and necessary and legitimate, why were they sold to us solely as anti-terrorism measures? Why has the Administration refused to acknowledge that the Patriot Act is being used against myriad crimes, from low-level stuff to serious violations?

Rest assured, this power grab was meant from the beginning to apply across the board. After all, most provisions of the Patriot Act had been written well before 9/11, but they couldn't get passed due to Congress-critters who were concerned about that quaint relic called the US Constitution. These blocked measures just needed the perfect excuse to become law. Along came 9/11… ⎇

33
THE GOVERNMENT OFFERED AROUND 30 REASONS FOR THE IRAQ INVASION

Just why did the US need to invade a militarily powerless Third World country on the other side of the globe? What could convince Americans to part with hundreds of billions of dollars and to send their sons and daughters to be killed, blinded, and mutilated? Obviously, just one reason wasn't going to do it. Neither would two or three. So the government, primarily members of the Bush Administration itself, trotted out around *30* reasons to invade and occupy an undeveloped country, kill and injure tens of thousands of civilians, and throw gasoline on the fire of jihadists, while sacrificing lives, limbs, and money.

We know the big three:

• Because Iraq possessed biological and chemical weapons, which the US had sold to Saddam in the 1980s and which Saddam destroyed in the late 1990s. Well in advance of the invasion, chief UN weapons inspector Hans Blix plainly stated that the WMD were gone. After the war, chief US weapons inspector David Kay — a Republican hand-picked by the Bushies to find the WMD — also declared that the stockpiles don't exist. He said that anyone who clings to the notion of their existence is "really delusional," also telling reporters: "I think it's most important that the president of the United States recognizes that in fact the weapons are not there."

• Because Iraq supported al Qaeda, even though no evidence of this connection has ever been found and, in a virtually ignored press conference, Bush flat-out admitted that Iraq was not involved in 9/11. (Tony Blair, at the conference with Bush, immediately backed him up on this point. Powell admitted the same thing in February 2002.) In summer 2004, the 9/11 Commission and the Senate Select Committee on Intelligence put what should be the final nails in the coffin, each body issuing a report bluntly declaring that there has never been a working relationship between Saddam and al Qaeda. Meanwhile, terrorist-supporting states such as Pakistan are considered America's great friends.

• Because Saddam was a dictator who oppressed the Iraqi people. This is true, but let's not forget that the Administration expresses no interest in "liberating" oppressed people in dozens of other tyrannies, such as Cuba, Burma, the Democratic Republic of Congo, China, Swaziland, and Sudan. Now that the WMD have proven to be vaporware, and the Iraq/Qaeda connection has been shot down, this "for the Iraqi people" excuse has retroactively become the dominant one. But even megahawk Paul Wolfowitz, the Deputy Secretary of Defense, has stated that this "by itself, as I think I said earlier, is a reason to help the Iraqis but it's not a reason to put American kids' lives at risk, certainly not on the scale we did it."

Aside from the big three, all inoperative, over two dozen other justifications popped up. The list below contains many — but not all — of the justifications that University of Illinois student Devon M. Largio scrupulously documented in her headline-making political science thesis on this topic:

• Whether or not Saddam had WMD, he *wanted* them.
• Iraq may have been involved in the anthrax mailings right after 9/11.
• The US should've deposed Saddam during the 1991 Gulf War.
• Iraq is weak and could be easily trounced.

- Iraq is a danger to the entire world and everyone in the world.
- Iraq is a threat specifically to the US.
- Iraq is a danger mainly to its neighbors.
- Iraq hasn't upheld UN resolutions.
- Saddam Hussein is an evil man.
- Attacking Iraq would spread democracy and capitalism throughout the Middle East.
- We don't know what Iraq's intentions are.
- It would send a message to other countries about aiding terrorists.
- For the sake of children in the US and the world.
- Invading Iraq would lead to world peace.
- Iraq was trying to get or develop nuclear weapons.
- Iraq must be invaded in order to defend freedom.
- Saddam Hussein was violating international law (by developing WMD).
- Because of the way history will judge us.
- Because Saddam hates the US.

As hard as it is to believe, the well of reasons hasn't yet run dry. When drumming up support for the Iraq attack, Bush twice mentioned that Hussein had allegedly tried to assassinate the first President Bush in April 1993. At a political fundraiser in Houston, late in September 2002, Bush said: "After all, this is the guy who tried to kill my dad." This has struck some observers as the most honest statement explaining Bush's burning desire to smack down Hussein.

Then we have the obvious reason for the war: to gain control of oil. No Cabinet-level member of the Administration said this in public, but President Bush's top economic adviser did.

In September 2002, Lawrence Lindsay enthused to the pro-war *Wall Street Journal*:

"When there is a regime change in Iraq, you could add three million to five million barrels [of oil per day] of production to world supply. The successful prosecution of the war would be good for the economy."

Undersecretary of Commerce Grant Aldonas said much the same thing, that invading Iraq "would open up this spigot on Iraqi oil which certainly would have a profound effect in terms of the performance of the world economy for those countries that are manufacturers and oil consumers."

While debating an energy bill on June 15, 2004, the Chairman of the House Energy and Commerce Committee, Republican Rep. Billy Tauzin, said:

"We are in dire need of a policy that tells the energy future traders on Wall Street to quit running the prices up and to begin thinking about a future where we are producing more energy at home for our own people instead of constantly fighting over battlefields to defend other people's energy supplies that we depend upon."

We mustn't overlook the much-circulated admission by Brigadier General William Looney, head of the US Central Command's Airborne Expeditionary Force. While talking to *Defense Week* about the no-fly zones over Iraq, he said: "It's a good thing, especially when there is a lot of oil out there we need."

And who could forget the "flypaper" rationale? In this bizarre scenario, America went to Iraq in order to draw all terrorists into that one country, where they could be conveniently dispatched, hopefully before blowing up or shooting too many US troops. Apparently, every terrorist in the world booked passage to Iraq, leaving not a single one available to attack Western interests elsewhere. Vice President Cheney was the main proponent of this fantasy, saying things like this on *Meet the Press*:

"So what we do on the ground in Iraq, our capabilities here are being tested in no small measure, but this is the place where we want to take on the terrorists. This is the place where we want to take on those elements that have come against the United States, and it's far more appropriate for us to do it there and far better for us to do it there than it is here at home."

Another reason for the invasion — this one largely unspoken — is the religious aspect: Christians versus infidels. Bush, as most everyone knows, is a hardcore fundamentalist who believes that he is directly doing God's bidding. The war against terror — in which Iraq is supposedly the primary battleground — is actually a holy war, not just to Mullah Omar, but to Bush as well. One indication is his famous use of the loaded word "crusade" to describe the battle.

Another example comes from a Bush cousin. For the widely overlooked book *The Bushes: Portrait of a Dynasty*, a Reagan hagiographer and his wife conducted unprecedented, candid interviews with many members of the Bush clan, leading Doug Wead — a former aide to both Presidents Bush — to remark: "The Schweizers have penetrated to the heart of the Bush family. This is as close as anyone has ever been able to get." A cousin who didn't want to be named opened up about the war on terror:

"George sees this as a religious war. He doesn't have a p.c. view of this war. His view of this is that they are trying to kill the Christians. And we as the Christians will strike back with more force and more ferocity than they will ever know."

Also part of the new crusade is Lt. Gen. William G. "Jerry" Boykin, the Deputy Undersecretary of Defense for Intelligence. When not leading the hunt for bin Laden and other top prizes in the war on terror, Boykin appears in full uniform in front of fundie gatherings and says things like: "We in the army of God, in the house of God, kingdom of God have been raised for such a time as this." When speaking of one of his Muslim adversaries, he thunders: "I knew my God was bigger than his. I knew that my God was a real God and his was an idol."

Another reason that has received almost zero public attention was proffered by Philip Zelikow, who at the time was on the President's Foreign Intelligence Advisory Board. This influential body monitors intelligence agencies — including the CIA, NSA, and Defense Intelligence Agency — and it reports directly to the President. Members have above top-secret security clearance, which allows them access to any classified information. As part of a panel at the University of Virginia on September 10, 2002 — right when the Administration started hard-selling the upcoming invasion — Zelikow said:

"Why would Iraq attack America or use nuclear weapons against us? I'll tell you what I think the real threat [is] and actually has been since 1990: It's the threat against Israel.

"And this is the threat that dare not speak its name, because the Europeans don't care deeply about that threat, I will tell you frankly. And the American government doesn't want to lean too hard on it rhetorically, because it is not a popular sell."

Three leading neoconservative architects of the invasion — Richard Perle, Undersecretary of Defense Douglas Feith, and David Wurmser (now the Vice President's Middle East Adviser) — used to be part of the Study Group on a New Israeli Strategy Toward 2000. In 1996, they released a paper called "A Clean Break: A New Strategy for Securing the Realm," which recommended that Hussein be removed as leader of Iraq, partly because this is "an important Israeli strategic objective in its own right" and partly because it would weaken Syria's ambitions.

Speaking of "selling" the war, a senior Administration figure openly admitted that this approach — attempting to convince Americans that it needed this invasion just like it needs detergent or Twinkies — was the operative one.

In early September 2002, White House Chief of Staff Andrew Card was asked why the Administration was starting to push its Iraq agenda so hard. He replied: "From a marketing point of view, you don't introduce new products in August." ▢

34
A LEADING PENTAGON HAWK ADMITTED THE IRAQ INVASION WAS ILLEGAL

Powerbroker Richard Perle was one of the prime movers behind the 2003 war on Iraq. He'd been pushing for it for more than a decade, since the original Gulf War.

This superhawk, known in the Beltway as the Prince of Darkness, was Reagan's Assistant Secretary of Defense, and he advised the first President Bush on foreign policy. He's heavily involved with two prime outlets of neo-conservative war-mongering — the Project for a New American Century and the American Enterprise Institute.

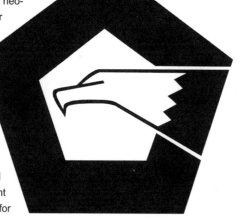

As the Chair of the influential, un-accountable Defense Policy Board — which advises the Defense Department's leaders — from 2001 to March 2003, he was in a perfect position to push for an Iraq attack. Not only did he have Rumsfeld's ear, he was backed by the number-two and number-three men in the Defense Department — Paul Wolfowitz and Douglas Feith — who for years had been jonesing to kick Iraq's ass. (Feith is the one who appointed Perle to the board.)

So it was very strange when Perle admitted that the war he fought so hard to start was illegal. Speaking in London at an event for the Institute of Contemporary Arts, he told the audience: "I think in this case international law stood in the way of doing the right thing." He groused that international law "would have required us to leave Saddam Hussein alone," something that Perle and his cohorts couldn't tolerate.

The London *Guardian* explains:

President George Bush has consistently argued that the war was legal either because of existing UN security council resolutions on Iraq — also the British government's publicly stated view — or as an act of self-defence permitted by international law.

But here we have the Pentagon's top adviser, who regularly appeared on TV to bang the drum for war, admitting that the US engaged in an illegal invasion.

As they say in Washington: Laws are for the little people. ▯

paragraphs in a Government Accountability Office report.

Homeland Security release concerns Operation Predator, a scheme to crack down on child
olesters. One part of the plan involves the database, which has been jointly created by the
epartment of Homeland Security's Bureau of Immigration and Customs Enforcement (which
uses the database), the FBI, the Secret Service, the Justice Department's Child Exploitation and
bscenity Section, the Postal Inspection Service, and the National Center for Missing and Exploited
ildren, with help from law enforcement agencies of other countries. The reasons are explained:

With its capacity to search and identify known images, the system is designed to help law enforcement agencies throughout the world identify and rescue children featured in the images. The system is also designed to facilitate prosecution of those who possess or distribute digital child pornography images in the wake of a 2002 Supreme Court decision (Ashcroft v. Free Speech Coalition) requiring proof that such images depict an actual child.

They say that "this system will eventually contain all known child pornography images."

35
THE US RUNS A NETWORK OF AT LEAST 20 SECRET PRISONS

Not too many things are more antithetical to constitutional and moral principles than secret prisons. Keeping prisoners incommunicado in remote, sometimes undisclosed facilities with no meaningful oversight brings to mind medieval dungeons, Star Chambers, and the Black Hole of Calcutta. Yet 21st century America has set up at least 20 such shadowy facilities. Some are officially admitted to exist, although we have next to no idea of what goes on inside, but authorities won't even concede the existence of some of the others. Both George W. Bush and State Department Coordinator for Counterterrorism Cofer Black have stated that at least 3,000 detainees have entered this subterranean network of off-the-books prisons.

The most well-known no-man's-land is at the Naval Base at Guantanamo Bay, Cuba. Originally, detainees were held in the outdoor Camp X-Ray; then they were moved to Camp Delta, built by Halliburton for an average cost of $47,550 for each 6-by-8-foot cell. The number of people held in this Caribbean gulag is usually given as somewhere around 600.

The other dark hole with the highest visibility is the Abu Ghraib prison near Baghdad, which dominated world headlines for weeks after *60 Minutes II* quit obeying the Pentagon and mustered the courage to broadcast photos of prisoners being beaten, abused, and sexually humiliated by giddy US military personnel.

The final facility with a somewhat high profile is the Collection Center located at the US Air Force

Base in Bagram, Afghanistan, which is said to be the primary detention center in that country. (The CIA has its own off-the-record hellhole in Bagram, plus another one — called The Pit — in Kabul.) Then there's the holding pen at Kandahar, supposedly just a way station for those headed to Bagram to enjoy the Air Force's hospitality. US Central Command has said that Afghanistan has many more facilities, as many as 20, that are just temporary stops on the road to Bagram, either directly or via Kandahar. The number of detainees is reportedly 300-something.

Iraq is home to a bare minimum of twelve detainment facilities run by the US military or the so-called Coalition. In addition to Abu Ghraib, the two big facilities are Camp Cropper and Camp Bucca, with smaller ones scattered about.

The only known Constitution-free detention center on US soil is the Consolidated Naval Brig in Charleston, South Carolina. It's home to two US citizens — José Padilla and Yaser Hamdi — who were held without legal recourse for two years before the Supreme Court half-heartedly stepped into the vicious battle over their fates. The brig also holds Qatar citizen Ali Saleh Kahlah al-Marri, who was originally indicted on fraud and vague terrorism charges through the normal justice process; just before trial, though, Bush declared him an enemy combatant, and he was whisked into the brig.

Numerous news articles focus on detention centers in Pakistan, but US authorities refuse to comment. The neither-confirm-nor-deny approach also holds for a reported CIA vacation spot in Jordan, the Al Jafr prison. On the other hand, the Pentagon specifically denies continued reports of captives being held at the US Naval base on the supremely remote island of Diego Garcia.

Human Rights First, the first group to tally all of these secret prisons, also notes [...] numbers of detainees — including "American Taliban" John Walker Lindh — have bee[...] short periods aboard US warships.

The group points out the Grand Canyon-size gulf between words and deeds: "In i[...] Reports on human rights conditions abroad, the US Department of State has c[...] criticized the practice of holding individuals incommunicado in secret detention faciliti[...]

36
THE GOVERNMENT HAS A DATABASE OF EVERY CHILD PORN IMAGE EVER MADE

The federal government has created a database that will eventually contain [...] pornography image ever created, from those in old Danish magazines to digital photo[...] to private pictures seized from busted pervs.

I'm reminded of the (probably) apocryphal tales of the Vatican's secret porn collec[...] be the largest in the world. In this case, though, it's true. The feds are building an[...] archive of kiddie porn, and it's remotely accessible (i.e., people physically located a[...] computers housing the database can still log into it).

They've been keeping quiet about such an important plan. The only mentions of t[...] come in a single paragraph in a press release from the Department of Homeland [...]

The GAO report concerns the use of peer-to-peer networks — best known for allowing users to swap unauthorized MP3s of corporate-controlled music — to share child pornography. Toward the end, the publication mentions the kiddie porn archive, confirming that it went live in January 2003, with the goal of the first phase being 100,000 images. It's "being populated with all known and unique child pornographic images obtained from national and international law enforcement sources and from CyberTipline reports filed with NCMEC."

Although housed at Customs, it "can be accessed remotely" by the agencies involved, including the nongovernmental National Center for Missing and Exploited Children.

In some ways, this sounds like a good idea, and the DHS claims that in its first six months, the system identified six kids in roughly 300 images. But putting all of this radioactively illegal, far-flung, extremely hard-to-obtain material into one place protected by just a password raises a whole raft of tough questions. Precisely who at each of these agencies will have access to this cornucopia of kiddie porn? How closely will access be monitored? How tight is the system's security? How often will passwords be changed? What happens if hackers compromise it? What are the implications of allowing a private organization to have access? What kind of oversight will there be? Public oversight has been nil, and by the time Congress was informed by the GAO, the database had already been a *fait accompli* for nine months. Let's hope that NAMBLA (the North American Man/Boy Love Association) doesn't have an accomplished hacker within its ranks. ⌑

37
PRESIDENTIAL DEBATES ARE STRICTLY CONTROLLED BY THE TWO MAJOR POLITICAL PARTIES

The great presidential debates of Lincoln-Douglas and Kennedy-Nixon have devolved into a canned photo-op where the candidates mouth platitudes, the same talking points we heard them parrot during the whole interminable campaign.

How did this happen? How did a free-spirited exchange of ideas, with gloves-off sparring between the opponents, become neutered and boring? In 1988, the two major parties realized that the debates were too un-predictable, too likely to harm a candidate. They weren't worth the risk. Something had to be done to turn them into stage-managed press conferences.

The national Republican and Democratic parties teamed up (again proving that they're just two sides of the same worthless coin) and created the Commission on Presidential Debates to control things. Comprised of operatives from both parties and funded by corporations, the CPD runs the show, having given the boot to the independent League of Women Voters.

This puppet on a string does the bidding of the Demopublican machine, virtually assuring that nothing threatening can happen to either major party candidate. As part of that mission, the CPD does everything it can to shut out third-party challengers. The CPD's director stated in 2002: "I think it's obvious that independent candidates mess things up."

Almost every aspect of the debates — where they will be held, who asks the questions, times for responses and rebuttals, whether the candidates may directly engage each other, who'll be in the audience, the height of the podiums — is dictated by the candidates. Representatives of both politicians sign a secret contract that spells out the terms in black and white. The CPD simply carries out these orders.

The nonprofit group Open Debates — which is attempting to put the debates under the control of a citizens' commission — has released leaked copies of these contracts. The 1996 agreement, for the debates between Clinton and Dole (and their veeps), said:

No follow-up questions by the moderator will be permitted, and no cross-questions by the candidates or cross-conversation between the candidates will be allowed under these rules.

Contracts for other years have had the same basic rules, which make for "debates" that are about as enthralling as watching paint dry.

Even the first President Bush admitted (after the fact): "It's too much show business and too much prompting, too much artificiality, and not really debates. They're rehearsed appearances." ☐

38
FOR OVER 100 YEARS, ALMOST EVERY DISCHARGE OF WASTE INTO US WATERS HAS BEEN ILLEGAL

We've all had a laugh over those ridiculous, unenforced laws that are still on the books, like the ones that forbid impersonating a wolf or buying a hat without a spouse's permission. But there are a few extremely important laws still in force that are lying around unused, rusting away from neglect. One of those laws is the Refuse Act, passed in 1899 as part of the Rivers and Harbors Act.

This federal law explicitly outlaws the chucking of refuse into a navigable body of water, which includes oceans, rivers, lakes, even wetlands, as well as the tributaries that feed any of them.

The one and only kind of waste that can be disposed of in this manner is the liquid gunk that already flows through the streets and sewers. If you want to toss *anything* else into the drink, there's only one way to legally do it: Get written permission from the Secretary of the Army, who first must get the nod from the Army Corps of Engineers. Needless to say, if anyone ever did do this, it hasn't been done in many, many decades.

A violation is considered a misdemeanor, the punishment being imprisonment for one to six months and/or a fine of up to $25,000 for each day the pollution occurs.

In 1966, the Supreme Court upheld the Refuse Act, specifying that it applied to industrial waste in addition to any other form of refuse (besides street/sewer runoff). From that time into the early 1970s, the law was brandished against such behemoths as US Steel, DuPont, and Standard Oil.

Then the Clean Water Act became law in 1972, and the legal situation — not to mention the nation's water — got a lot murkier. While the Refuse Act outlawed all dumping sans Army permission, the Clean Water Act tried to set up reasonable amounts, varying by industry, location, type of pollutant, etc. In other words, it gave corporations a whole lot of wiggle room.

In recent years, the Refuse Act has been dusted off and used on extremely rare occasions. In 1991, Exxon pled guilty to violating several laws, including the Refuse Act, for the *Valdez* disaster. The next year, the EPA reports: "Pipeline rupture caused an 860,000 gallon oil spill into the Mississippi, Gasconade, and Missouri rivers. Shell pleaded guilty to violation of the Refuse Act and agreed to pay $8,400,000 in fines, restitution, and settlements." In 1997, a small salvage company and its owner were busted under the Refuse Act and other federal laws for dumping crap into Maryland's Patapsco River.

Maybe the best part is that the statute gives a strong incentive for ordinary citizens to nail polluters. If you turn in a corporation or other entity that's fouling the water, and your information leads to a conviction under the Refuse Act, you get *half* of the fine levied. Even if the government won't pursue the charges, you can bring a case against the polluter in the name of the government in order to collect the dough.

The Refuse Act is still in force and has been blessed by the Supreme Court, so every discharge or dumping of waste without the Army Secretary's permission for over a century has been a federal crime. This includes everything from private boats that spew oil into a lake to broken pipelines, ruptured oil tankers, municipalities that discharge raw sewage, mines that dump fill, factory farms that dispose of animal waste, and, of course, factories and plants that toss the entire periodic table into our water.

The National Resource Defense Council noted in 2002: "Some 218 million Americans live within 10 miles of a polluted lake, river, stream or coastal area. About 45 percent of the nation's assessed waters are still unsafe for fishing, swimming or supporting aquatic life — up from 40 percent in 1998." That's an awful lot of Refuse Act violations.

39
THE WATER SUPPLY IS FILLED WITH SMALL AMOUNTS OF PHARMACEUTICALS AND OTHER CHEMICALS

Every time you wash your tub with a cleaner, rinse off make-up or suntan lotion, pour coffee down the drain, or flush old prescription drugs, small amounts of their chemical components end up in the water supply. Maybe the most surprising source of pollutants is our own waste. Whenever you go to the bathroom, you're excreting small bits of everything you take — all the prescription and illegal drugs, the caffeine and nicotine, the aspirin and cough medicine. With most of these substances, small portions make it out of your body unaltered or just slightly changed. Don't expect treatment to catch these nasties. The Environmental Protection Agency baldly declares: "No municipal sewage treatment plants are engineered for PPCP removal." ("PPCP" stands for "pharmaceuticals and personal care products.")

The EPA first discovered a pharmaceutical chemical in water in 1976, but the emphasis at the time was on industrial pollutants, so no one paid much attention to it. In the 1980s, Europe started studying this kind of contamination in earnest. The US got in on the act in the mid-1990s, but PPCP pollution is still under the radar. In fact, of the major environmentalism websites I checked, none of them discussed pharmaceuticals and other personal care products in our drinking water.

In 1999 and 2000, the US Geological Survey checked *agua* samples in 30 states, finding 82 types of this class of pollutant (they looked for 95). The median amount was seven, with one stream containing 38. Among the most common were cholesterol, steroids, caffeine, a fire retardant, a disinfectant, and an insect repellant. A 1998 survey of 40 German waterways found 31 drugs and five metabolites. These and other studies in the US, Canada, and Europe have found antibiotics, hormones (mainly from birth control pills), antidepressants, codeine, high blood pressure meds, antacids, ibuprofen, musks, Darvon (a synthetic opioid), nicotine metabolites, blood lipid regulators, and the radioactive stuff you drink before getting X-rayed. No one has yet tested for illegal drugs, but given their rate of use, they and their metabolites have to be part of the mix.

So there's no doubt that our water supply is swimming with microscopic portions of chemicals from dandruff shampoo, Viagra, and pot. The question is what kind of effect this is having on us and on aquatic life. Scientists involved with the issue frankly admit that we just don't know. When it comes to humans, researchers have yet to study in-depth the effects of these micro-doses. As far as fish and other aquatic beasties are concerned, until recently no one thought to study the effects. Who would've thought, as a 2003 study found, that fish in Texas would have Prozac in their brains and livers? Beyond that, the studies that are done look at the effect of just one chemical, but in the real world these chemicals are occurring in combinations, resulting in cocktails with perhaps unknowable effects.

A hydrologist with the US Geological Survey, Sheila Murphy, summed up the problem as pointedly as anyone could: "It doesn't just go down the toilet and into Neverland." ⌁

40
WELL OVER 300,000 TONS OF CHEMICAL WEAPONS HAVE BEEN DUMPED INTO THE SEA

Industrial waste and drugs aren't the only water waste we need to worry about. For decades, the world's oceans were used as a giant garbage can for the most noxious, lethal chemicals in existence. Countries have dumped hundreds of thousands of tons of weapons loaded with cyanide, mustard gas, sarin, phosgene, VX, Zyklon B, and other nerve agents into the drink.

Such dumps started around the time of the first World War, but documentation of this early activity is practically nonexistent. The practice kicked into overdrive in the immediate aftermath of WWII. Faced with huge stockpiles of Germany's weapons, the Allies pitched them into the waters around Europe. NATO officially estimates that from 1945 to 1947, 300,000 tons of these weapons — containing 60,000 tons of nerve agents — were heaved into the Baltic and the North Atlantic.

Japan had much less of this stuff than the Nazis, but still almost 5,000 tons were cast into the Pacific. Britain and Australia used this method to dispose of some of their own arsenals after hostilities ended. Dumps in the 1950s continued to be primarily of WWII-vintage nerve agents. In the late sixties and 1970, the US jettisoned tens of thousands of its own leaky, sarin-loaded M-55 rockets into the Atlantic.

The *Bulletin of the Atomic Scientists* reports:

In all, the United States is responsible for 60 sea dumpings totaling about 100,000 tons of chemical weapons filled with toxic materials, according to a 1993 study by the US Arms Control and Disarmament Agency (acda). The US sites are located in the Gulf of Mexico, off the coast of New Jersey, California, Florida, [New York] and South Carolina, and near India, Italy, Norway, Denmark, Japan, and Australia.

Russian scientist Alexander Kaffka warns: "There were some important safety rules envisaged at the time; for instance, to dump only in deep waters and far from the shores. But the rules were often broken, which led to the most dangerous kind of dumping — at shallow depths, in straits, and in areas of active fishing."

Mustard gas bombs have washed up on beaches in Poland, Germany, and Australia, and several people in Japan have been killed, with dozens injured, after coming into contact with surfaced nerve agents. Danish fisherman have netted weapons hundreds of times. Some of the ordnance was known to have been leaking before it was sent to the ocean floor, and no one doubts that corrosion has allowed more of the material to escape its containers. The *New York Times* reports: "Scientists from the Baltic countries and Russia have found lethal material mixed in with sediments, and highly toxic sulfur mustard gas, transformed into brown-yellow clumps of gel, has washed ashore."

Still, there's vast disagreement over how much of a threat this material presents. Obviously, most governments think everything's A-OK. The US hasn't even sent a probe to look at the condition of dumped chem-weapons since 1974, and it has no plans to check them ever again. Scientists tend to be more concerned, but some of them caution that doing anything with such huge amounts of poison is riskier than just leaving it alone. ☐

41
CIGARETTE BUTTS ARE THE MOST COMMON TYPE OF LITTER

I don't think I'm alone in becoming so inured to seeing cigarette butts on the ground that I no longer notice them. To our jaded eyes, they blend seamlessly into the landscape, an expected part of the surroundings.

And no wonder. In Westernized countries, they're the most common form of litter; every other piece of trash chucked in public places is the filtered end of a cigarette. The journal *Tobacco Control* estimates that each year over 4.5 *trillion* end up as litter (over 250 billion in the US alone). Add cigarette packs and their cellophane wrappers to the stew, and the situation becomes even worse.

Big Tobacco is eager to foster the belief that their butts are biodegradable, but no study has shown that it takes less than a year for a butt to break down. In fact, some argue that they never truly disintegrate because the filter component is made of cellulose acetate, a form of plastic which never completely goes away.

Besides being an eyesore, the butts are an environmental hazard. Most will eventually get swept into the water supply, where the hundreds of chemicals they contain will be leached out. Fish, seabirds, and other marine creatures have been known to gobble them up, mistaking them for food. If they don't outright poison the critter, they block its digestive and excretory systems. Then there are the kids who nosh on them. It's a relatively small number of children, to be sure, but those illnesses and deaths are preventable. As are the fires caused by flung butts.

Preventing cig litter isn't high up on the tobacco industry's list of priorities, though. They refuse to take many easy steps to help. For one thing, they could put "don't litter" messages on their packages, both in words and with pictograms (a person tossing trash into a wastebasket). Come to think of it, there's nothing stopping them from stamping a message like that on each and every cancer stick they make. Phillip Morris USA has recently said that it puts such messages on "select" packs, which begs the question — why not on *all* packs?

Another action not taken by the industry is to aggressively distribute "personal ashtrays," small, pocket-size receptacles for holding cigarette butts. For a while, RJ Reynolds would send a free pack of thin, foil-lined personal ashtrays to anyone who requested it, but for reasons never explained, they suddenly stopped. The website CigaretteLitter.org writes: "It has long been clear that RJR had no interest in this program being successful as they never promoted it and always made sure they ran out of ashtrays on a frequent basis."

Indeed, if the industry were serious, it could enclose one of these wafer-thin ashtrays in every pack of coffin nails. Or it could sell little plastic devices, about the size of a cigarette lighter, to serve the same purpose, if only they'd design and market them with the same zeal as the cigs themselves. Like the lighter itself, these little disposal units could become an ubiquitous part of the smoker's paraphernalia. Lighters could even have these little ashtrays built in.

Why won't the smoking industry take these and other solid steps? The answers are revealed in internal documents. A Philip Morris memo from March '98 addresses the issue, stating the company's "business objective":

Minimize emergence of regulations resulting in product bans or *committing the Company to take financial and logistical mandated responsibility for disposal of its products and/or packaging.*

An internal report from the Tobacco Institute, the leading industry group, two decades prior says: "Our best course of action may be maintaining a low profile while working to exempt cigarettes from coverage of pending litter control legislation." It recommends that "the concept of courtesy should be limited to the smoking of — rather than the disposal of — tobacco products." The plan notes that "'no-litter' campaigns might be useful; but they should not be implemented before cost/benefit and political analysis has been completed." Researcher Anne Landman of the American Lung Association explains: "[The] document shows that the industry believed that by backing any fees or taxes to help clean up cigarette litter, they would be buying into the 'social cost' argument against smoking."

Of course, when push comes to flick, it's the smoker who tosses the butt on the ground. Those who don't want to contribute to the problem can use public ashtrays or buy pocket versions, such as the pen-shaped, brass "Smart Ashtray" or the colorful, plastic "BUTTsOUT." ⌷

42
CAVIAR INVOLVES EXTRAORDINARY CRUELTY

It's no secret that meat comes to us through a process of savage cruelty. For those who care to look, the atrocities inflicted on cows, pigs, chickens, turkeys, and other such creatures are well documented. But one product that often escapes notice is caviar.

True, people consume a lot more hamburgers than fish eggs, but caviar can be found in the refrigerated section of many grocery stores, not to mention every one of the gourmet and "world food" stores that dot most cities. Like fast food joints, though, they're not anxious for us to know how their product got to their shelves.

If you thought that sturgeon nicely laid their eggs somewhere for divers to harmlessly scoop up, forget it. Instead, imagine grabbing a pregnant woman off the street, pimpslapping her, slicing her belly open, ripping out her fetus, then leaving her to slowly die of her injuries and blood loss. That's the human analogy to caviar.

In his investigation of the seedy, greedy worldwide caviar industry, Simon Cooper gives an eyewitness account of a poacher in the Caspian Sea harvesting eggs from the "thick, writhing carpet" of sturgeon he's caught:

The poacher selects a fat female. She is about four feet long and swollen with eggs. He hits her hard with a plank of wood — not hard enough to kill, but enough to stun. Blood trickles from her eyeballs, mouth, and gills. Quickly, the poacher rolls her over, slits open her belly, reaches inside, and carefully extracts a plump, gray-black sac about the size of a pillow. He puts the egg sac into a large plastic bucket and throws the eviscerated fish on the ground, where she flaps and thrashes, her abdomen gaping, until she succumbs and dies. ☐

43
THE HIPPOCRATIC OATH HAS BEEN CHANGED DRAMATICALLY

In almost every medical school when the would-be docs graduate, they recite the Hippocratic oath, pledging to help the sick and behave ethically. This solemn vow, in use since ancient Greek times, is named after the physician Hippocrates, father of Western medicine, although it probably wasn't written by him.

But a Hippocratic oath taken today is not the original oath. While some of the broad ideals are the same, several of the original requirements have been dropped. Originally, the Hippocratic oath was sworn before several gods. You'll occasionally find a contemporary version that invokes one god, but most of them do away with all references to supernatural beings.

Most controversially (to us moderns, anyway), the true oath forbids doctors from performing euthanasia and abortions:

I will neither give a deadly drug to anybody who asked for it, nor will I make a suggestion to this effect. Similarly I will not give to a woman an abortive remedy.

Another section puts the kibosh on hooking up with patients (and, it seems to imply, with patients' family and friends):

Whatever houses I may visit, I will come for the benefit of the sick, remaining free of all intentional injustice, of all mischief and in particular of sexual relations with both female and male persons, be they free or slaves.

Reflecting the Greek system of a mentor imparting medical knowledge to his pupil, the original oath also binds physicians to their teachers for life. If the teacher is ever strapped for cash, his protégé must fork it over. If the teacher has sons, the pupil must regard them as brothers and give them a medical education for free.

Almost all modern versions, including the AMA-approved rendition, do away with these inconvenient precepts. The documentary program *NOVA* reports:

According to a 1993 survey of 150 US and Canadian medical schools, for example, only 14 percent of modern oaths prohibit euthanasia, 11 percent hold covenant with a deity, 8 percent foreswear abortion, and a mere 3 percent forbid sexual contact with patients — all maxims held sacred in the classical version. ✄

44
MOST HYSTERECTOMIES ARE UNNECESSARY

In a hysterectomy, a doctor carves out the uterus and usually the cervix (40 percent of the time, the ovaries are also taken) to deal with a number of conditions ranging from cancer to fibroids to severe PMS. The second-most popular surgical procedure on women, hysterectomies are performed 600,000 times per year in the US. Stanley West, MD, calculates: "At that rate, one out of every three women in this country will have had a hysterectomy by the time she reaches her sixtieth birthday."

The problem is, 70 to 90 percent of the time, the surgery is unnecessary.

For a study published in the journal *Obstetrics and Gynecology*, researchers eyed the cases of 497 women who had undergone the operation. They assembled a panel of physicians who are experts in various specialties to judge whether the procedure was appropriate in each case. The results were dismal: 70 percent of the hysterectomies shouldn't have been done.

Then the researchers judged the operations based on the guidelines set down by the American College of Obstetricians and Gynecologists, and the outcome was even worse: 76 percent of the operations were deemed "inappropriate." The researchers write: "The most common reasons recommendations for hysterectomies [were] considered inappropriate were lack of adequate diagnostic evaluation and failure to try alternative treatments before hysterectomy."

Dr. West, a division chief at St. Vincent's Hospital in New York, goes even further, stating that 90 percent are unnecessary. The operation must be done in cases of uterine cancer, which account for 10 percent of hysterectomies. But, the doc says, every other hysterectomy-inducing disorder can be treated with other, less drastic techniques that avoid or greatly lessen the repercussions of uterus removal — namely, sterility (always), depression, memory loss, and other psychological problems (often), lack of sex drive and response (often), heart disease (increased risk), and death (twelve out of 10,000 women die from the procedure).

Uterine fibroids — the cause of a third of hysterectomies — can be cut out individually, if they truly need to be removed at all. Endometriosis, cysts, pain, abnormal bleeding, PMS, uterine prolapse (in which the uterus loses support and heads south), and pelvic inflammatory disease can be treated by surgeries other than hysterectomies, drugs, alternative therapies, and/or other methods.

Dr. West laments:

The surprisingly outdated attitudes doctors harbor toward female patients are a big part of the problem. Some very old-fashioned views remain embedded in medical training. It may take a few more decades and more medical consumerism on the part of women before the old attitudes give way to a more rational and scientific basis for hysterectomy. ⌑

45
USING SUNSCREEN CAN CAUSE CANCER

It's easy to think that slathering on sunscreen will make you practically invulnerable to skin cancer. Those evil rays will just bounce off you à la Superman. The manufacturers of these products don't exactly go out of their way to let you know that this isn't the case.

Most sunscreens only block the ultraviolet rays known as UVB, which cause sunburn and, in the long term, some skin cancer. But they do very little, next to nothing, to filter out the longer UVA rays, which also trigger skin cancer (in fact, UVA is probably more likely to do so). In other words, while you are prevented from being fried like a lobster, other rays that cause serious long-term health problems are pounding your skin unabated.

Often, wearing sunscreen only makes things worse, because people tend to stay outside longer when they think they're protected by coconut-scented body armor. Thus, they drink up more of the killer UVA.

And let's not forget that it's absolutely crucial for us to get Vitamin D, which is formed when our bods are exposed UVB, the very wavelength being stopped in its tracks by sunscreen. Among other things, D protects against some cancers, including breast and colon.

To drive another nail into sunscreen's coffin, be aware that when you use it, you're smearing loads of chemicals, some toxic, onto your skin, which drinks them up like soda and pipes them right into your body.

So what's a Sun worshipper to do? Ditch the lotions altogether. Spend small amounts of time in the Sun until your skin acclimates and you're able to stay exposed longer — an hour a day — without turning red. If you have to be outside longer, use clothing and things like beach umbrellas to keep the excess rays off your skin. Dr. Joseph Mercola boils it down: "The key is to never burn."

46
INVOLUNTARY HUMAN EXPERIMENTATION IS NOT A THING OF THE PAST

A study conducted by Johns Hopkins University, published in the *Journal of Medical Ethics*, asked hundreds of "health researchers in developing countries" if their studies using human subjects were being screened by ethics boards. The findings were bleak: 44 percent of respondents said that no one reviews their use of human guinea pigs. Of these unchecked experiments, US corporations and nonprofits fund one-third. Regarding the studies that were reviewed, in 92 percent of the cases, the ethics board of the institution performing the experiment did the screening, with no input from higher-level bodies. The study unearthed another fundamental problem — cases in which the patient consent forms weren't in the host country's language.

Not that all researchers even bother with consent forms. In the past few years, India has been roiled by revelations of several illegal drug trials that resulted in deaths. Some of the country's largest biotech and drug-manufacturing companies are neck-deep in scandals involving elderly people, sterile women, and cancer patients all being given experimental drugs without their knowledge. (In the cancer case, the secret trials were performed for a researcher at Johns Hopkins).

But undeveloped countries are hardly the only sites of Mengelean medical ethics. Pediatric drug testing on orphans in the US has almost completely escaped public scrutiny, but independent investigative reporter Liam Scheff is lifting the lid. (Due to their utter powerlessness, orphans have always been favored lab rats for medical experimentation.) ICC — a Catholic charity under the auspices of the Archdiocese of New York — houses children who tested HIV-positive or who were born to mothers with HIV. These kids have been guinea pigs for dozens of drug experiments funded by government agencies and pharmaceutical companies. They're given extremely toxic drugs, such as AZT, sometimes while they're still in the crib.

While some involved parties claim that the kids are simply being given wonderful cutting-edge drugs, documents obtained by the London *Observer* show that some trials have tested the "safety and tolerance" and "toxicity" of HIV drugs and the "tolerance [and] safety" of herpes drugs. The *Observer* reports that an "experiment sponsored by Glaxo and US drug firm Pfizer investigated the 'long-term safety' of anti-bacterial drugs on three-month-old babies." One study is titled, "The Safety and Effectiveness of Treating Advanced AIDS Patients between the Ages 4 and 22 with Seven Drugs, Some at Higher than Usual Doses." Children who refuse to take the drugs have a hole surgically drilled into their abdomen, so that the meds can be shunted directly into their bodies. ⌂

47
HEAD TRANSPLANTS ON MONKEYS HAVE ALREADY BEEN PERFORMED

The successful transplant of a primate's head from its own body to that of another must rank as one of the greatest medical achievements of the twentieth century, if not all time. Even if it didn't usher in a brave new world of head/brain/body transplants for humans, it would surely be embedded in the mass mind like Dolly the cloned sheep. But that isn't how it happened.

Dr. Robert White — at the time, a neurosurgeon at Cleveland's Metro Health Care Center — experimented with keeping disembodied monkey and dog brains alive during the 1960s. In 1970, he upped the ante by severing the head of a rhesus monkey, then attaching it to the headless, still-living body of a second monkey. An article from London's *Sunday Telegraph Magazine* sets the scene of the 18-hour surgery:

Chalk marks on the floor fixed the positions of more than thirty highly drilled professionals: two surgical teams, a squad of anaesthesiologists, assorted nurses, phalanxes of technicians, a bevy of scientists equipped to analyse blood and urine samples on the spot.

The poor creature regained consciousness and, according to White's paper in *Surgery*, it and the subsequent Frankenmonkeys were well aware of their surroundings, visually tracking people and objects. Traumatized beyond all comprehension, they were also agitated and violent, chomping a staff member's finger "if orally stimulated." In her death book *Stiff*, Mary Roach writes:

When White placed food in their mouths, they chewed it and attempted to swallow it — a bit of a dirty trick, given that the esophagus hadn't been reconnected and was now a dead end. The monkeys lived anywhere from six hours to three days, most of them dying from rejection issues or from bleeding.

Although this amazing and troubling procedure initially generated headlines, it's been largely forgotten. In the past few years, isolated articles on White's work have popped up in the British mainstream media and the American alternative press (*Wired* and the *Cleveland Scene*, for example). But this seemingly impossible feat failed to become common knowledge.

White caught a lot of heat from bioethicists, fellow doctors, and animal rights activists. This, plus the expense of these operations, meant that he had to give up this field of research. Still, during his occasional interviews, he dreams of pulling the ol' switcheroo on human noggins. Several countries less prone to hand-wringing have expressed interest, he says, but the funding just isn't there. And who wants to be the first head on the chopping block? The procedure would be of most benefit to paralyzed people whose bodies are in danger of giving out. Because medical science still can't reconnect severed spinal nerves, any recipient would be unable to move below the neck. Once the people in white coats overcome this limitation, White could find himself back in business. And heads will roll. ☐

Dr. White isn't the only scientist who's been playing musical heads. Optometrist and anatomist Paul Pietsch has fricasseed salamanders — their brains, heads, and eyes — in every conceivable combination. Not as impressive as higher primates, but the results have been at least as good. Pietsch has successfully attached an embryonic head to the eye socket of a young salamander. The second head became sentient, but the host croaked after a few months.

Another poor amphibian, charmingly nicknamed Brainless, had its entire brain (except for the medulla oblongata) carved out of its head. He survived by being force-fed but naturally was never again active.

Then there was Punky, the salamander who was given the brain of a frog. As theorized, the little guy quit snarfing up tiny worms — a salamander delicacy — and instead lived peaceably with them, as frogs do.

48
SCIENTISTS ARE RECREATING
THE 1918 SPANISH FLU VIRUS

The year from spring 1918 to spring 1919 saw one of the worst epidemics — perhaps even *the* worst — in human history. The Spanish flu raced around the globe, killing 20 to 50 million people. That's a higher body count than World War I. More than the "Black Death" in medieval Europe. The Human Virology website at Stanford University explains:

An estimated 675,000 Americans died of influenza during the pandemic, ten times as many as in the world war. Of the US soldiers who died in Europe, half of them fell to the influenza virus and not to the enemy. ...

The effect of the influenza epidemic was so severe that the average life span in the US was depressed by 10 years. The influenza virus had a profound virulence, with a mortality rate at 2.5% compared to the previous influenza epidemics, which were less than 0.1%.

The *Encyclopedia Britannica* avers: "Outbreaks of the flu occurred in nearly every inhabited part of the world..." Some people died less than 24 hours after catching the bug. Oddly, it was most likely to cut down young adults, rather than the usual targets of influenza — children and the elderly.

Coughs and Sneezes Spread Diseases

As Dangerous as Poison Gas Shells

SPREAD OF SPANISH INFLUENZA MENACES OUR WAR PRODUCTION

U. S. Public Health Service Begins Na-tion-wide Health Campaign.

You get the idea — it was a worldwide catastrophe that could've easily caused societies to crumble. Thank goodness it could never happen again. Well, that's actually not a sure thing. Not content to leave well enough alone, scientists are in the process of *recreating* the Spanish flu virus.

Dr. Jeffrey Taubenberger from the US Armed Forces Institute of Pathology found portions of the killer in tissue samples from the time period. He and his colleagues were able to decode several genetic sequences, which they published.

Taking it to the next level, they teamed up with other scientists to partially resurrect the virus. In 2001, they spliced a gene from the 1918 flu into a run-of-the-mill flu virus. The next year, they did the same trick, only this time they added two 1918 genes into the mix. The resulting patchwork virus killed mice at a much higher level than current strains. The Sunshine Project, a watchdog organization fighting the development of biological weapons, warns: "This experiment is only one step away from taking the 1918 demon entirely out of the bottle and bringing the Spanish flu back to life."

Why take such a huge risk by reanimating a defunct killer of millions of people? The scientists have varying explanations. To study influenza in general. To figure out what made this virus so deadly and if it could happen again. To develop a vaccine against the 1918 virus (which no one would need if the virus weren't brought back in the first place). Simply because the scientists wanted to test out some new techniques, and, as Taubenberger told the American Society for Microbiology: "The 1918 flu was by far and away the most interesting thing we could think of..." Yet another reason was to keep the Institute's massive collection of 60 million tissue samples from being tossed out as a cost-cutting measure. Taubenberger: "Everyone was bending over backwards to see what part of the government they could cut away next, so I want to make my own little contribution and point out why it would be prudent to keep this place in business."

While those first two goals are worthwhile in theory, we might sleep more soundly if they were approached in different ways. Couldn't scientists just examine the genetic code without actually cooking up the virus? Won't computer simulations work? If you trust that harmful viruses don't escape from labs, you haven't read the Department of Agriculture Inspector General's report on lax conditions at facilities housing these nasty beasts. This 2003 tongue-lashing said:

Security measures at 20 of the 104 laboratories were not commensurate with the risk associated with the pathogens they housed. These 20 laboratories represented over half of the laboratories in our sample that stored high con-

sequence pathogens. Alarm systems, surveillance cameras, and identification badges were commonly lacking in buildings housing the laboratories, and key-card devices or sign-in sheets were not generally used to record entries to the laboratories.

It gave this reassuring example:

We discovered a Centers for Disease Control and Prevention (CDC) select agent at one institution that was kept in an unsecured freezer and for which no risk assessment had been made. The agent, Yersinia pestis, causes bubonic and pneumonic plague and requires strict containment. The freezer that stored this agent had not been inventoried since 1994, when a box of unidentified pathogens was already noted as missing.

Hmm, I'm feeling a little feverish.…

49
THE VATICAN, INCLUDING THE POPE, IS DIRECTLY INVOLVED IN THE CATHOLIC CHURCH'S PEDOPHILE COVER-UP

It took several decades, but in 2002 the media finally gave due attention to the epidemic of priests who molest children and the higher-ups who transfer the perps to other dioceses, where they choose from a fresh crop of potential victims. The press was rightly unsparing when it came to naming priests, bishops, archbishops, and cardinals in the US, but that courage didn't extend past America's borders. Except in exceedingly rare instances, the media couldn't work up the nerve to point fingers at the Vatican. Despite this conspicuous blind spot, several unearthed documents directly implicate the highest levels of the Catholic Church, including three Popes, in the cover-up.

The earliest such document — "Instruction on the Manner of Proceeding in Cases of Solicitation" — was sent to every high-ranking cleric in the world in 1962 (it was uncovered during legal action in 2003). It explains what to do when a priest gets accused of sexual acts with a penitent (someone whose confession they'd heard), a child, or an animal. The gist is that the offending man of the cloth is to be secretly tried by local Church officials (or, in some cases, the Vatican's Holy Office). Secular authorities are not to be alerted, and all paperwork is to be walled up in the diocese's "secret archive."

The "Instruction" includes a secrecy clause regarding these transgressions — an oath to be recited in which the cleric swears "under the pain of excommunication" and "other most serious penalties" that he will "observe this secret absolutely and in every way," never "directly or indirectly" revealing anything, "even for the most urgent and most serious cause [even] for the purpose of a greater good."

A note at the end of the main body declares that the "Instruction" was issued by "the most eminent Cardinal Secretary of the Holy Office" and was personally approved by Pope John XXIII.

Priest James Porter pled guilty to molesting 28 children during the 1960s and early 1970s (the actual count is believed to be around 100 kids in five states). Documents show that his superiors, fully aware of his serial child-rape, shuffled him to one diocese after another. In 2002, a *Boston Herald* lawsuit forced the release of Porter's file. It turns out that the pedo-priest had written a letter directly to Pope Paul VI in 1973, confessing his molestations and asking the Pontiff to let him out of the priesthood. It's not known how the Pope responded, but the next year Porter was no longer a priest. It wasn't until 20 years later that many of his victims banded together and got him sent to prison. Although they undoubtedly were aware of earlier cases, this provides documentary proof that the highest levels of the Vatican knew what was happening by 1973, at the latest.

The most recent smoking document proving the Pope's awareness and complicity dates back just a few years. (It too was publicly released during the scandal of 2002.) Dated May 29, 1999, the order signed by Pope John Paul calls for the defrocking of Robert Burns, a priest who pled guilty to indecent assault of a child. In it, his Holiness says that the molester "ought to live away from the places where his previous condition is known." However, wrote the Pope, the diocese doesn't have to ship him elsewhere "if it is foreseen that the presence of the suppliant will cause no scandal."

Lawyer Roderick MacLeish, who handles sex abuse lawsuits against the Church, told Reuters:

"For the first time we've seen documents from the Vatican that emphasize the word that we've seen so often here in Boston — 'scandal.' This document says he is to be relocated to another place where presumably they wouldn't know about him, unless the bishop or the cardinal of the appropriate diocese determines it will cause no scandal. What about the children?" ♡

50
GOD'S NAME IS "JEALOUS"

There's an old joke that says God's name is Harold, as in: "Our Father, who art in Heaven, Harold be thy name…"

The strange thing is, that's not too much off the mark, only the truth is even weirder. The LORD does indeed have a name, kind of like Andrew or Beth or José.

It's right there in the Bible, at Exodus 34:13. Moses has trudged up Mount Sinai with a second pair of stone tablets, on which God will write the Ten Commandments. Moses and the Big G engage in some repartee, then God says:

"For thou shalt worship no other god: for the LORD, whose name is Jealous, is a jealous God"

This is straight out of the King James Version. God reveals "his" own name: Jealous.

In the original Hebrew, the key words in this verse are *shem* and *qanna'*. According to one of the standard reference works in this area — *A Concise Dictionary of the Words in the Hebrew Bible* by James Strongs — *shem* is a noun meaning "name." One of its specific denotations is "the Name (as designation of God)." The word *qanna'* means "jealous" and is applied only to God.

Other English translations say the same basic thing as the King James Version. The New International Version gives it as: "Do not worship any other god, for the LORD, whose name is Jealous, is a jealous God." The English Standard Version phrases it parenthetically: "(for you shall worship no other god, for the LORD, whose name is Jealous, is a jealous God)." The New International Readers Version gives God a more relaxed feel: "Do not worship any other god. I am a jealous God. In fact, my name is Jealous."

Why isn't this mentioned in Sunday school? Perhaps because it could lead to children pledging, "One nation, under Jealous," people cursing, "Jealous damn it!" or the government stamping on currency: "In Jealous we trust."

But if you're going to accept the Bible, then you have to accept it when God reveals his own name, no matter how odd or silly.

May Jealous have mercy on my soul. ♡

REFERENCES

Male Clits. Blackledge, Catherine. *The Story of V: A Natural History of Female Sexuality*. Rutgers University Press, 2004. § Gray, Henry. *Anatomy of the Human Body*. 20th ed., rev. and re-edited by Warren H. Lewis. Philadelphia: Lea & Febiger, 1918. § Sevely, Josephine Lowndes. *Eve's Secrets: A New Theory of Female Sexuality*. Random House, 1987.

False Dads. American Association of Blood Banks. "Annual Report Summary for Testing in 1999." No date. § American Association of Blood Banks. "Annual Report Summary for Testing in 2001." Oct 2002. § Baker, Robin. Ph.D. *Sperm Wars: The Science of Sex*. HarperCollins, 1996. § Child Support Analysis website. "Misattributed Paternity." 5 July 2004. [www.childsupportanalysis.co.uk]. § Gallagher, Caoilfhionn. "In the Name of the Father? Legal and Ethical Dilemmas Surrounding 'Accidental' Findings of Non-Paternity." Annual Conference 2003, Socio-Legal Studies Association at Nottigham Law School. [www.nls.ntu.ac.uk/slsa2003/]. § Lucassen, Anneke and Michael Parker. "Revealing False Paternity: Some Ethical Considerations" *Lancet* 357 (2001): 1033-5. § Philipp, E. "Discussion: Moral, Social and Ethical Issues." *Law and Ethics of A.I.D. and Embryo Transfer*. Ciba Foundation Symposium (Vol. 17), G.E.W. Wostenholme and D.W. Fitzsimons (eds.). Amsterdam: Elsevier, Excerpta Medica, North-Holland, 1973: 63-66.

Old Porn. *1000 Nudes: Uwe Scheid Collection*. Benedikt Taschen, 1994. § Cooper, Emmanuel. *Fully Exposed: The Male Nude in Photography* (second ed.). Routledge, 1995. § Coopersmith, Jonathan. "Pornography, Technology and Progress." *Icon* 4 (1998). § Nazarieff, Serge. *Early Erotic Photography*. Benedikt Taschen, 1993. § Nazarieff, Serge. *Stereo Akte/Nudes/Nus*. Benedikt Taschen, 1993. § Neret, Gilles. *Erotica Universalis*. Benedikt Taschen, 1994. § Simons, G.L. *The Illustrated Book of Sexual Records*. 1974, 1982, 1997-2001. Online version at [www.world-sex-records.com]. § Website of Barcelonan artist Daniel Verdejo [www.arterupestre-c.com]. § Kinsey Institute website [www.kinseyinstitute.org].

Shakespeare. Macrone, Michael. *Naughty Shakespeare*. Andrews McMeel, 1997. § Partridge, Eric. *Shakespeare's Bawdy* (fourth edition). Routledge, 2001. Originally 1947.

Barbie. Lord, M.G. *Forever Barbie: The Unauthorized Biography of a Real Doll.* William Morrow and Company, 1994. § Doll Reference: Vintage Dolls 1951-1976. [members.tripod.com/ltanis/]. § Dolls and Toys Australia. [www.dollsandtoysaustralia.com].

Fetuses. Blackledge, Catherine. *The Story of V: A Natural History of Female Sexuality.* Rutgers University Press, 2004. § Edell, Dean. *Eat, Drink, and Be Merry: America's Doctor Tells You Why the Health Experts Are Wrong.* HarperCollins, 1999: 209. § Giorgi, G, and M. Siccardi. "Ultrasonographic Observation of a Female Fetus' Sexual Behavior in Utero." *American Journal of Obstetrics and Gynecology* 175 (Sept 1996): 753. § Meizner, I. "Sonographic Observation of in Utero Fetal 'Masturbation'." *Journal of Ultrasound Medicine* 6.2 (Feb 1987): 111. § Taylor, Timothy. *The Prehistory of Sex: Four Million Years of Human Sexual Culture.* Bantam, 1996: 282.

Legal Highs. Erowid website. [www.erowid.org]. § Lycaeum website. [www.lycaeum.org].

DEA Ruling. Randall, R.C. (editor). *Marijuana, Medicine and the Law,* Volumes I and II. Galen Press, 1988 and 1989. The two volumes present testimony and documents from the DEA's hearings.

Drug Warnings. US Food and Drug Administration. "Safety-Related Drug Labeling Changes" on the page "Medical Product Safety Information." FDA website [www.fda.gov].

SUVs. Bureau of Transportation Statistics, US Department of Transportation. "National Transportation Statistics 2003." March 2004. [www.bts.gov]. § Harborview Injury Prevention and Research Center at the University of Washington. "Light Trucks Pose Greater Injury Risk to Pedestrians" [press release]. 15 June 2004.

Aristotle. Asimov, Isaac. *Isaac Asimov's Book of Facts.* Fawcett Columbine Books, 1979. § Kaisler, Denise. "Comet Misconceptions." Undated paper on doctoral student Kaisler's site on the website of UCLA's Division of Astronomy and Astrophysics [www.astro.ucla.edu/~kaisler/]. § Wilson, Prof. Fred L. "Science and Human Values: Aristotle." Undated paper on Dr. Wilson's site on the Rochester Institute of Technology website [www.rit.edu/~flwstv/]. § "Aristotle." "Atom." "Democritus." *Encyclopedia Britannica*.

Native American Slaves. Bailey, L.R. *Indian Slave Trade in the Southwest*. Tower Publications, 1966. § Gallay, Alan. *The Indian Slave Trade: The Rise of the English Empire in the American South, 1960-1717*. Yale University Press, 2002. § Perdue, Theda. "Slavery." Entry in *Encyclopedia of North American Indians*. Frederick E. Hoxie, ed. Houghton Mifflin Company, 1996.

Washington's Graft. A Calm Observer. "A Calm Observer." In *Shaking the Foundations: 200 Years of Investigative Journalism in America*. Bruce Shapiro, ed. Thunder's Mouth Press and Nation Books, 2003.

Declaration Slur. Texts of the US Declaration of Independence and the original California Constitution of 1879. § Manheim, Prof. Karl. "Discrimination against Chinese in California." Undated paper on Dr. Manheim's site on the Loyola Law School website [class.lls.edu/~manheimk].

Audubon. Hart-Davis, Duff. *Audubon's Elephant: America's Greatest Naturalist and the Making of* The Birds of America. Henry Holt and Company, 2004. § May, Stephen. "John James Audubon: Squire of Mill Grove and Genius of Art and Science." *Pennsylvania Heritage Magazine*. Reprinted on jjaudubon.com. § "John James Audubon." *Encyclopædia Britannica*. 2004. § "John James Audubon 1785-1851." National Audubon Society website [www.audubon.org].

Lynchings. Carrigan, William D. "The Lynching of Persons of Mexican Origin or Descent in the United States, 1848 to 1928." *Journal of Social History*, Winter 2003. § Zangrando, Robert L. "About Lynching." *The Reader's Companion to American History*. Eric Foner and John A. Garraty, eds. Houghton Mifflin, 1991. § "Georgia Lynching Victims." *Atlanta-Journal Constitution* website [www.ajc.com], 16 May 2002. § "Lynching." The Handbook of Texas Online [www.tsha.utexas.edu].

Freud. Crews, Frederick, ed. *Unauthorized Freud: Doubters Confront a Legend*. Penguin Books, 1999. Especially the following chapters: "Anna O.: The First Tall Tale" by Mikkel Borch-Jacobsen; "Delusions and Dream in Freud's 'Dora'" by Allen Esterson; "Exemplary Botches" by Frank J. Sulloway; "A Little Child Shall Mislead Them" by Joseph Wolpe and Stanley Rachman; Crews' "Overview" of Part III.

Monopoly. Anspach, Ralph. *The Billion Dollar Monopoly Swindle: The True Story Behind Monopoly*. Self-published, 1998. § Anti-Monopoly website [www.antimonopoly.com]. § Monopoly website [www.hasbro.com/monopoly/].

Gandhi. Chadha, Yogesh. *Gandhi: A Life*. John Wiley & Sons, 1997: 395-7. § Payne, Robert. *The Life and Death of Mahatma Gandhi*. Smithmark Publishers, 1995: 501-6. § Both of these books, although sympathetic to Gandhi overall, cover many of his warts. For a no-hold-barred look at his hypocrisies, see *Gandhi: Behind the Mask of Divinity*.

Americans in Concentration Camps. Bard, Mitchell G. *Forgotten Victims: The Abandonment of Americans in Hitler's Camps*. Westview Press, 1994.

Nuke Accidents. CNN. "US Nuclear Bomb 'on Seabed off Greenland'." CNN website, 13 Aug 2000. § Environment, Safety and Health, US Department of Energy. "Palomares, Spain Medical Surveillance and Environmental Monitoring Program." [tis.eh.doe.gov/health/]. § Tiwari, Jaya, and Cleve J. Gray. "US Nuclear Weapons Accidents." Center for Defense Information website [www.cdi.org]. § United Press International. "Nuclear Near-Disaster Reportedly Covered Up." *Sun-News*, 11 June 1979. § US Nuclear Weapons Cost Study Project, Foreign Policy Studies Program. "The Palomares "Broken Arrow," January 1966" Brookings Institution [www.brook.edu]. § "List of Nuclear Accidents." Wikipedia [wikipedia.org]. § "Nuclear Accidents" section on Nuclearfiles.org.

Missile Code. Blair, Bruce G. "Keeping Presidents in the Nuclear Dark (Episode #1: The Case of the Missing 'Permissive Action Links')." Center for Defense Intelligence website [www.cdi.org], 11 Feb 2004.

Land Giveaway. Environmental Working Group. "Who Owns the West?" [report]. 2004. [www.ewg.org/mining].

Corporate Tax Evasion. General Accounting Office. "Comparison of the Reported Tax Liabilities of Foreign- and U.S.-Controlled Corporations, 1996-2000." Feb 2004. GAO-04-358. § McKinnon, John D. "Many Companies Avoided Taxes Even as Profits Soared in Boom." *Wall Street Journal*, 06 April 2004: A1.

Discharge Codes. Associated Press. "Pentagon Abolishes Code on Discharges of Military Misfits." *New York Times*, 23 Mar 1974. § Kihss, Peter. "Use of Personal-Characterization Coding on Military Discharges Is Assailed." *New York Times*, 30 Sep 1973. § The American War Library website [members.aol.com/veterans/]. This site used to list the meanings for hundreds of SPN codes, but at some point it removed this information.

Homeless Vets. Stewart, Jocelyn Y. "From the Ranks to the Street." *Los Angeles Times*, 29 May 2004. § National Coalition for Homeless Veterans website [www.nchv.org]. § US Department of Veterans Affairs website [www.va.gov].

Prison Population. Bureau of Justice Statistics, Office of Justice Programs, US Department of Justice. [www.ojp.usdoj.gov/bjs/]. § Research Development and Statistics Directorate, UK Home Office. "World Prison Population List" (fourth edition), 2003. [www.homeoffice.gov.uk/rds/]. § November Coalition website [www.november.org].

Asset Forfeiture. Fishburn, Mike. "Gored by the Ox: A Discussion of the Federal and Texas Laws That Empower Civil-Asset Forfeiture." *Rutgers Law Record*, 26.4 (2002). § Asset Forfeiture Program, Department of Justice website [www.usdoj.gov/jmd/afp/]. § Executive Office for Asset Forfeiture, Department of Treasury website [www.treas.gov/offices/eotffc/teoaf/]. § Forfeiture Endangers American Rights website [www.fear.org]

EPA. Jenkins, Cate, PhD. "Comments on the EPA Office of Inspector General's 1/27/03 Interim Report Titled: 'EPA's Response to the World Trade Center Towers Collapse.'" Environmental Protection Agency, 04 July 2003. § Office of Inspector General, US Environmental Protection Agency. "EPA's Response to the World Trade Center

Collapse: Challenges, Successes and Areas for Improvement." 21 Aug 2003. Report #2003-P-00012. § Smith, Sam. "9/11 Memo Reveals Asbestos 'Cover-up'." *New York Post*, 16 July 2004. § Press releases on the EPA website [www.epa.gov].

Condoleezza Rice. Central Intelligence Agency. "Bin Ladin Determined to Strike In US." President Daily Brief, 6 Aug 2001. Released 10 Aug 2004. Widely published in the media. § Transcript of Rice's testimony before the National Commission on Terrorist Attacks Upon the United States, 8 April 2004. Published on the websites of CNN and NYT, among others.

Al Qaeda. Congressional Research Service. "Terrorist Attacks by al Qaeda." 31 March 2004. Posted on the House Committee on Government Reform Minority Office website [www.house.gov/reform/min/].

Patriot Act. Lichtblau, Eric. "US Cautiously Begins to Seize Millions in Foreign Banks." *New York Times*, 30 May 2003. § Lichtblau, Eric. "Patriot Act Goes Beyond Terror." *New York Times*, 28 Sept 2003. § Murphy, Kevin. "8-Year Sentence for Radio Interference, UW Grad's Actions Labeled Terrorism." *Capital Times* (Madison, WI), 13 May 2004. § Unsigned. "Hauling Cash Lands Man In Jail." AlaNews Network, 23 Dec 2003. § US Department of Justice. "Report from the Field: The USA PATRIOT Act at Work." July 2004. § Preserving Life and Liberty website [www.lifeandliberty.gov].

Iraq Reasons. Cooper, Richard T. "General Casts War in Religious Terms." *Los Angeles Times*, 16 Oct 2003. § Unsigned. "US Expert Slams WMD 'Delusions'." BBC, 5 June 2004. § Transcript of *Meet the Press* [TV show], 14 Sept 2003. § Largio, Devon M. "Uncovering the Rationales for the War on Iraq: The Words of the Bush Administration, Congress, and the Media from September 12, 2001 to October 11, 2002." Thesis for the Degree of Bachelor of Arts in Political Science, College of Liberal Arts and Sciences, University of Illinois, Urbana-Champaign, Illinois. 2004. § King, John. "Bush Calls Saddam 'the Guy Who Tried to Kill My Dad'." CNN, 27 Sept 2002. § Mekay, Emad. "Iraq War Launched to Protect Israel - Bush Adviser." Inter Press Service, 29 Mar 2004. § "Deputy Secretary Wolfowitz Interview with Sam Tannenhaus, *Vanity Fair*" [transcript]. Department of Defense website, 09 May 2003 [www.dod.gov]. § "Quotation of the

Day." *New York Times*, 07 Sept 2002: A6. § *Congressional Record — House*, 15 June 2004: H4117, H4120. § Harnden, Toby. "Ousting Saddam 'Would be Good Business'." *Daily Telegraph* (London), 17 Sept 2002. § Moran, Michael, and Alex Johnson. "Oil After Saddam: All Bets Are in." MSNBC, 7 Nov 2002. § Schweizer, Peter, and Rochelle Schweizer. *The Bushes: Portrait of a Dynasty*. Doubleday, 2004.

Illegal War. Burkeman, Oliver, and Julian Borger. "War Critics Astonished as US Hawk Admits Invasion Was Illegal." *Guardian* (London). 20 Nov 2003. § Perle's biography on the American Enterprise Institute website [www.aei.org].

Secret Prisons. Human Rights First. "Ending Secret Detentions" [report]. June 2004. § Aldinger, Charles. "Halliburton to Build New Cells at Guantanamo Base." Reuters, 27 July 2002. § Bartelme, Tony. "The Navy's Secret Brig." *Post and Courier* (Charleston, SC), 23 Nov 2003.

Child Porn Database. General Accounting Office. "File-Sharing Programs: Users of Peer-to-Peer Networks Can Readily Access Child Pornography. Statement of Linda D. Koontz, Director, Information Management Issues." 09 Sept 2003. GAO-03-1115T. § Department of Homeland Security. "Fact Sheet: Operation Predator." 09 July 2003.

Presidential Debates. Open Debates website [www.opendebates.org].

Water Dumping. Office of Compliance, Office of Enforcement and Compliance Assurance, US Environmental Protection Agency. "Profile of the Ground Transportation Industry: Trucking, Railroad, and Pipeline." Sept 1997. EPA/310-R-97-002. § Office of Enforcement and Compliance Assurance, US Environmental Protection Agency. "Enforcement and Compliance Assurance Accomplishments Report FY 1997." July 1998. EPA-300-R-98-003. § US Code, Title 33, Chapter 9, Subchapter 1, Sections 407 & 411.

Drugs in Water. Kolpin, DW, *et al.* "Pharmaceuticals, Hormones, and Other Organic Wastewater Contaminants in US Streams, 1999-2000: A National Reconnaissance." *Environmental Science and Technology* 36.6 (2002): 1202-11. § Morson, Berny. "Test Finds Boulder Creek Is Potpourri of Chemicals." *Rocky Mountain News* (Denver, CO), 29 Oct 2003.

§ National Ground Water Association. "Proceedings of the 2nd International Conference on Pharmaceuticals and Endocrine Disrupting Chemicals in Water, October 9-11, 2001, Minneapolis, Minnesota." NGWA, undated. § Stiles, Nikki. "The Mystery Behind PPCPs." *Small Flows Quarterly* 5.1 (winter 2004). § US Environmental Protection Agency. Pharmaceuticals and Personal Care Products (PPCPs) as Environmental Pollutants website [www.epa.gov/nerlesd1/chemistry/pharma/].

Chemical Weapons. Defence Publishing Service, Department of Defence (Australia). "Chemical Warfare Agent Sea Dumping off Australia" (revised and updated edition). 2003. § Hogendoorn, E.J. "A Chemical Weapons Atlas." *Bulletin of the Atomic Scientists* 53.5 (Sept/Oct 1997). § Simons, Marlise. "Discarded War Munitions Leach Poisons Into the Baltic." *New York Times*, 20 June 2003.

Cigarette Butts. Unsigned. "Cigarette Butts Cause Environmental Pollution." Reuters, 24 May 1999. § Anne Landman's Collection at Tobacco Documents Online [tobaccodocuments.org/landman/]. § BUTTsOUT website [www.buttsout.net]. § Cigarette Litter website. [www.cigarettelitter.org]. § Smart Ashtray website [www.smartashtray.com].

Caviar. Cooper, Simon. "Caviar." *SEED Magazine*, Nov 2003: 93-101, 125-9.

Hippocratic Oath. Website of the *NOVA* episode "Survivor M.D.," from the Public Broadcasting System, March-April 2001. [www.pbs.org/wgbh/nova/doctors/]. The original oath quoted is the 1943 English-language translation by Ludwig Edelstein.

Hysterectomies. Bouchez, Colette. "Hysterectomy: The Operation Women May Not Need." ABCNews.com, 11 Dec 2002. § Broder, Michael S., MD, *et al*. "The Appropriateness of Recommendations for Hysterectomy" [abstract]. *Obstetrics & Gynecology* 2000;95:199-205. § West, Stanley, MD, with Paula Dranov. *The Hysterectomy Hoax: The Truth About Why Many Hysterectomies Are Unnecessary and How to Avoid Them* (third edition). Next Decade, Inc., 2002.

Human Experimentation. Barnett, Antony. "UK Firm Tried HIV Drug on Orphans." *Observer* (London). 4 April 2004. § Basu, Indrajit. "India's Clinical Trials and Tribulations." *Asia Times*, 23 July 2004. § Hyder, A.A., *et al.* "Ethical Review of Health Research: A Perspective From Developing Country Researchers" [abstract]. *Journal of Medical Ethics* 2004;30:68-72. § Johns Hopkins University Bloomberg School of Public Health. "Ethical Review of Research in Developing Countries Needed" [press release], 24 Feb 2004. § Scheff, Liam. "The House That AIDS Built." AltHeal website [www.altheal.org], Jan 2004.

Sunscreen. Cedric F. Garland. "More on Preventing Skin Cancer." *British Medical Journal*, 2003;327:1228 (22 November). § Thompson, Larry. "Sunscreen, Skin Cancer, and UVA." HealthLink (Medical College of Wisconsin), 26 July 2000. [healthlink.mcw.edu]. § Mercola.com, website of Dr. Joseph Mercola.

Head Transplants. Bennun, David. "Dr. Robert White." *Sunday Telegraph Magazine* (London), 2000. Reprinted at the author's website [bennun.biz]. § Roach, Mary. *Stiff: The Curious Lives of Human Cadavers*. Norton, 2003. § **Sidebar**: ShuffleBrain, the website of Paul Pietsch, PhD [www.indiana.edu/~pietsch].

Spanish Flu. Billings, Molly. "The Influenza Pandemic of 1918." Human Virology website, Stanford University [www.stanford.edu/group/virus/]. § Davies, Pete. *Devil's Flu: The World's Deadliest Influenza Epidemic and the Scientific Hunt for the Virus That Caused It*. Owl Books, 2000. § *MacNeil/Lehrer NewsHour*. "Revisiting the 1918 Flu" [interview]. Public Broadcasting System, 24 Mar 1997. § Office of the Inspector General, US Department of Agriculture. "Controls Over Biological, Chemical, and Radioactive Materials at Institutions Funded by the US Department of Agriculture" [audit report]. Sept 2003. 50099-14-At. § The Sunshine Project. "Recreating the Spanish Flu?" [briefing paper]. 9 Oct 2003. [www.sunshine-project.org].

Pedo-Priest Cover-up. The Supreme and Holy Congregation of the Holy Office. "Instruction on the Manner of Proceeding in Cases of Solicitation." The Vatican Press, 1962. § Barnett, Antony. "Vatican Ordered Bishops Worldwide to Cover up Priests' Sex Abuses." *Observer* (London), 17 Aug 2003. § Unsigned. "Sex Policy Order a 'Smoking Gun'

Pointing at Vatican." Reuters, 12 Dec 2002. § Sullivan, Jack. "Medeiros, Vatican Involved in Coverup." *Boston Herald*, 16 May 2002.

God's Name. Various translations of the Bible. § *A Concise Dictionary of the Words in the Hebrew Bible* by James Strongs. Online at Blue Letter Bible [blueletterbible.org].

Note: An index for this book is available at books.disinfo.com